WHAT OTH ~~ABOUT~~
THE MISEDUCATION OF THE BLACK CHILD

"... solutions for the crisis in American education that is keeping millions of Blacks from achieving their potential in society and life."
— *Ebony* Magazine's Book Shelf

"The Hares advocate Black-directed education...taking us back to the landmark successes of the back-woods, one-room schoolhouse experience with a million new ideas to combat racism, poverty and class imperialism."
— Dr. Gwendolyn Goldsby Grant,
Essence Magazine columnist

"A lot of insights you shared in the Miseducation of the Black Child really struck a responsive cord in me."
— Terrance Newton
Elementary school teacher, member of Parents Notebook

"These strategies are guaranteed to fly, guaranteed to work, because they also programmatically help the home and the community and society in turn to influence the school."
— *The New York Amsterdam News*

"For years now Drs. Nathan and Julia Hare have been in the vanguard of Black thought...but what impresses me most [in *The Miseducation*] is their discussion on what we can do as individuals and as a community to improve matters...Must reading."
— Leon Dixon, W.E.B. DuBois Learning Center

"The Hares indicate that 'a role model without a success role is like a castrated stallion facing a herd of wild mares, inspired and excited but without internal motivation sufficient to actualize, manifest or consummate the magnitude of the inspiration.'"
— *The Chicago Defender*

"...Some people have the wheel, some have the horse-drawn carriage, some have the combustible engine, but *The Miseducation of the Black Child* is the automobile, the Cadillac."
— *The Norfolk Journal and Guide*

"...we concur, "if the simmering anti-public school sentiment continues to gather steam, no amount of wailing about the sacredness and
inviolable but fading benefits of a public school system will suffice."
- *The Miami Times*

"The Hares maintain that the solution will not rest in improving teaching methods (we've already got too many techniques"). They see the
battle being won increasingly outside the classroom, or what they call
'the classworld'".
- *The Michigan Chronicle*

"Not since Paulo Freire's *The Pedagogy of the Oppressed* has a book been
so heralded in progressive educational circles. *The Miseducation of the
Black Child* will become a textbook on inner city education. It pulls no
punches."
- Edgar Ridley, Management Consultant,
Ridley & Associates

"The Miseducation of the Black Child is the most provocative, profound, and schematically advanced program for the education and
uplift of Black folk since Carter G. Woodson's seminal work, The
Miseducation of the Negro...*The Miseducation of the Black Child* should
be a ready-reference and guide for every Black or African American
religious, social and civic organization in America...I am greatly
impressed with the logic and simplicity of the plan, and the manner
and style it is written."
- Talmadge Anderson, founding editor
of *The Western Journal of Black Studies*

"...novel approach contains the potential for regenerating a moribund
public school system and providing literacy to every Black man,
woman and child."
- Robert Staples, sociologist, UCSF

"The Hares lay the plan for Africans to solve our own educational
problems and take charge of our own destiny...Powerful...Should be in
every American household...a breakthrough."
- *Your Black Books Guide*

"A much-needed and well-constructed design for improving education in the public schools."
- Dr. Maulana Karenga, originator of *Kwanzaa*,
and Chair of Black Studies at Long Beach

THE HARE PLAN
To Overhaul the Public Schools
and
Educate Every Black Man,
Woman and Child

by
Nathan Hare, Ph.D.
and
Julia Hare, Ed.D.

Banneker Books

THE HARE PLAN

To Overhaul the Public Schools
and
Educate Every Black Man,
Woman and Child

ISBN: 0-9613086-4-8
Published by
BANNEKER BOOKS
1801 Bush St., Suite 118
San Francisco, California 94109

Dedication

To the staff of Slick, Oklahoma's little Toussaint L' Ouverture High, which fell to racial integration in the late 1950's — Mildred Foshee, Auzzie Garrett, Sylvester and Willa Combs — for turning Nathan from a psychological dropout of the schools of San Diego into something of an intellectual; to New Haven's Rev. Dr. E.R. Edmonds, who as Dean of Men at Oklahoma's Langston University, compelled him to continue that journey; and for the inspiration of Langston's late great poet Melvin Tolson.

To Tulsa's George Washington Carver Junior High School and Booker T. Washington High (for giving Julia an unforgettable and uniquely formative experience); and to Mrs. Edna Gray, late principal of the Truesdell (college-controlled) Laboratory School in Washington, D.C., for her special confidence in Julia's teaching abilities and for nominating and encouraging her to win a District of Columbia competition for educator of the year for all grade levels and all races in the nation's capital.

CONTENTS

v

Decentralization and Deregulation
Sex Education
Dropout Rates
Teen Unemployment
Teachers Attitudes and Expectations
Lack of Motivation
Money
Curriculum
Teacher and Staff Development
Dress Code
The Spanking Taboo
An Epilogue to Misconceptions

Part I

The Problem

Chapter 1

Reveille for the Public Schools

Everybody is talking about it, in both private and public places. It is no secret now that public schools are failing black children.

People spice their conversations with newsmedia accounts of intransigent mass inner city school pathology. The public psyche is bombarded almost daily with deplorable test score results, school violence and official investigations, interspersed with grand and lofty foundation "commission" reports that chronicle the incipient decline and demise of the American educational system — especially for black citizens.

On city buses, casual observers decry the boisterous public demeanor of black school children. Black children dropping out of school to dot crowded street corners and drug-infested playgrounds are officially tallied every day. Parents who can afford to do so are searching for alternatives, including sending their children to high-priced private schools.

However, the relative success of private schools can be attributed more to a built-in selectivity of students (for example, more affluent and adjusted and/or more involved and motivated parents impacting students) than any inherent difference in what private schools and their public school peers are doing.

In any case, nobody much is able now to deny the black child's impending educational decimation. Joined by complaints of many public school educators themselves, advocates involved in the noisy cacophony of arguments and disagreements are locked in a brinksmanlike quandary over the way in which the black child's education — indeed the existing educational system — can be salvaged; sometimes whether it can be saved at all.

It is in this context that we (a former prizewinning public school teacher and a sociologist turned clinical psychologist, with over a quarter of a century's involvement in black educational reform from coast to coast) offer this handbook to teachers, parents, leaders, educators and others who desire to save the black child and — arguably a quickly evaporating possibility — the public school system itself.

Many serious leaders, thinkers and observers, are giving up on this "raisin in the sun." In Milwaukee, Wisconsin, for instance, black militant leaders, personified by Democratic State Representative Annette Polly Williams, joined conservative white Republicans in a Parental Choice Program based on school vouchers. Also in Milwaukee, a black city councilman has warned of violence and "armed struggle" if the white powers-that-be do not correct the devastation of black children within five years. In the words of an old African proverb, "it takes strong medicine to cure a strong disease."

Accordingly, out of the apathetic and repressive ashes of two decades (the 1970s and the 1980's) the Farrakhan rejuvenated Nation of Islam is ressurecting its highly regarded elementary schools. Private conversations with Minister Farrakhan reveal plans to extend the Nation of Islam's educational system to the college and university levels in the not too distant future. Additionally, there is a fullblown secular "independent black school" movement sufficient to generate and sustain a national organization at a moment's notice.

Rumors of Black Secession from the Public Schools

Already there is talk of a need to move black children out of public schools. We know disenchanted individual parents who have resorted to keeping their children home and teaching them themselves — very well.

We have witnessed some of these children. One afternoon we sat amazed and heard two black children, a boy and a girl about ten and eleven years old in a black nationalist ultra-afrocentric family, demonstrate more knowledge of classical European literature than the overwhelming majority of black college students can.

If the simmering anti-public school sentiment continues to gather steam, no amount of wailing about the sacredness and inviolable but fading benefits of a public school system will suffice. Even the black middle class is streaming out of the central city to private and suburban schools. Teachers themselves, when they desire to move up, tend to consider moving out of impoverished schools a virtual necessity — the farther out the better. In any case, when once they have demonstrated a modicum of innovation and superiority in the classroom, they typically are transferred out of the slums to teach middle class children (often white). This is the popular direction of routine teacher promotions.

Conversely, victims of demotions, or those up for early retirement, will often be sent back to schools of the black poor areas, what they call "the cemetery." On the other hand, good black teachers unable to present rigid central city credentials may frequently find work in white suburban districts or even white "alternative" schools within the city.

Chapter 2

Who Are the Children?

Living under the care and guidance of adults who themselves are socioeconomically defeated and cannot own or operate their own corner stores, categorized, labeled and miseducated by alien practitioners from the suburbs, black children of the inner city (called "handicapped," "uneducable," "at risk," and "underclass") frequently impress the public imagination with a dazzling composition and memorization of rap lyrics and athletic strategies. They create and dictate the popular fads and fashions in music and dance, from breakdancing to rapping, to dunking and stylized athletics. Many go on, still in their teens or postadolescence, to develop and dominate the inner city drug market at a level of social organization and economic capability that rivals and sometimes stymies the police force and the bureaucratic corporate marketplace. And they do this in the face of horrific social opposition and illegitimization.

Increasingly today, black inner city youth emerge as volatile powderkegs of variegated social and physical threats of terror after dark to adults both black and white. Labeled educationally "at risk," they nevertheless affect upscale middle class suburbia and present imponderable dilemmas that stir constitutional waters on the cutting edge of grownup social conflict and civil liberties. They appear instinctively to anticipate and provoke needed redefinitions and reforms in the range of legal and social tolerance. Growing up and sometimes thriving in divergent ways amid homicidal danger and self-destruction, they present themselves, at about the age of four or five to ambivalent public schools.

There, fearing the unfamiliar but anticipating some unknown beginning, they enter the arms of white and black middle class adult individuals who have abandoned the children's residential neighborhoods. These adult middle class "caretakers," "guidance counselors," "principals," "superintendents" and "board members" return to the children's "underclass communities" with apprehension and often resentment during the daily freeway rush hours to make their livings ministering to these children of the "underclass" they try to persuade to be like them and to follow their views, values, behavior and manners.

In the most fundamental sense, these inner city black children are called upon to become white persons in black bodies, compelled to learn to see the world through what W.E.B. DuBois called "dual lenses" — one black, the other white.

However, merely to point that out in this era of the "crossover," or the "rainbow," in which we live today is to risk being labeled a "black racist" or some kind of "radical," so sinister is the unwritten social imperative for blacks to identify with whites, that is to say, as whites.

In this world of we-are-all-one make-believe, blacks who cannot or will not assimilate are rejected and set apart, sometimes jailed, as "unassimilated" or "incorrigible." Early in their school lives, they may be labeled "hardcore," "at risk," or "socially maladaptive" and assigned to the socioeconomic scrapheap before

8

they can get off the educational ground.

We recognize that (for most poor children) public school education may be about all they will ever have. We know there is much benefit in saving the concept of public-funded education on the face of it, although this is not necessarily indentical to retaining the public school system as it now stands in America. There is no need to save public schools if they are not worth saving.

The Black Male Child: Products of a Broken Patriarchy

With black boys especially, we are dealing with the products of a broken patriarchy. In a patriarchal racism, it is the male who poses the primary threat to the ruling male, who in his mind can take his place in the bedroom and the boardroom. Hence a white oppressor must take special pains to suppress the black male. If you kill the male, you do not have to worry about the female and the children, as they are bound to wither away. This is not sexual chauvanism but a biosocial reality.

You can make all black women millionaires, and the problems of the race would increase. If the black male is not brought along simultaneously (as he was not in the 1970s and 1980s), the black female will look around and find that she has no male to stand beside her and that she is further isolated psychologically and sociologically from her male.

Under such a circumstance, as early as 1969, we continually warned, the male will feel threatened and unable to contend with the female; the female will have contempt and low respect for the male; and the children will grow up unable to respect their fathers.

Unable to respect their fathers, they cannot respect other authority figures: their leaders, their teachers, or their preachers.

Girls will grow up ambivalent and unable to fully respect their male counterparts or to make and sustain a satisfactory love adjustment; boys, seeing their mates as extensions of their one-parent or dominant mothers, will fight out unresolved conflicts with their mates in adulthood love life. Male and female alike, they must live as children unable to fully respect themselves.

After turning against themselves, they turn against their parents and authority figures, then finally against society itself, gripped by self-destruction and sociopathy. They will lack the psychological and social integrity to imagine and negotiate what mental health practitioners call a "success identity."

All of this is compounded in the case of impoverished black children, rejected in their corporeality, their physiognomy, the way they look, their psychophysiological beings, so recently descended from ritual segregation and rejection as well as chattel slavery. This is at bottom the difference between African-Americans and the frequently heralded "model immigrants" who have come thousands of miles to America to make their mark, that is to say, their market. They have been self-selected for the success struggle before they reached these shores.

Therefore, we must take special pains to find ways to give inner-city African-American children — and, in the process as we proceed, to give the black race or the black community — a success identity.

Black children frequently have no clear, positive, or realistic adult ambition. They wish to succeed, but have no clear notion of how or what that will entail for them. On top of this, they will experience other difficulties in finding a "success role," let alone related goals to strive and work for in the achievement of that role. For one thing, there is a paucity of adults with the experience to advise them. What they see around them is a lot of failure in the black community. When they do venture out or otherwise witness success, the feeling is that it leaves them out, does not apply to them.

We can begin to change that by such strategies as mobilizing parents and other members of their families, groups of them (to offset their apprehensions and reluctance and to comprise a bigger impact) to come to the school and do things.

We also must get community people to do what they can do. We must not only bring the role models to the school, we must find ways to get them involved in the schools, get community people to do what they can do; not only the stars but the mundane role model as well.

We must stop seeing none other than stars as role models, then complaining that black children take only stars as role models. By focusing on glittering role models, we are left too often not with role models but with models playing roles. In fact, it may be more efficacious as well as more feasible to focus on persons in the child's own environment, or at least to include persons from their world and social spheres.

We must start with where the children are, then teach them functions that are germane to their reality (including such things as negotiating with the welfare institutions and other agencies and entities which might be alien to the middle class). We also must connect them to *people* who are germane to their world and not just people acceptable to the middle class.

Not so long ago, teachers in the rural South, where most

blacks resided prior to the era of "integration" and pressures for assimilation, teachers enjoyed a reverence that rivaled a hybridization of the doctor and the pastor. Now we have irreverence not only for the teacher and the pastor but also for the parents.

Psychiatrist William Glasser speaks of "failure activities" or activities that are dysfunctional for the child. Black psychologists such as Janice Hale-Benson, in *Black Children: Their Roots, and Cultural Learning Styles* has described tendencies in the black boy to turn away from the home at a certain age (approximately coincidental to the Freudian "masculine protest") and seek his values and behavioral codes in the street. These street skills, knowledge and values will frequently prove dysfunctional in later adulthood life as well as in the school.

Recently a black boy who said he always wanted to be on the "America's Most Wanted" television program shot into an apartment and accidentally killed a four-year-old boy. Aside from taking him to a psychologist, somebody might have ushered him to a free acting class at the local YMCA or wherever and set him to learning how to act so he might someday portray those on the "America's Most Wanted" show.

This boy's experience also points up the fact that the black community must be filled with workshops and the preparation of careers and career goals as forceful as Barry Gordy's budding Motown in the lives of such artists as Diana Ross and the Supremes and Marvin Gaye.

Parents who are already motivated and involved must be employed (perhaps paid) to motivate their peers, their neighbors, relatives and friends. Children who are already motivated can be organized to motivate their peers and neighbors and friends, including adults, as well.

We hear a lot about ''at risk'' children but nothing about at risk parents or at risk communities. We must find ways to lessen the risk of each category of victims or at-risk persons. Short of eliminating poverty and oppression and other broad societal problems, we must find ways to lessen the antagonism between at-risk parent and child as well as at-risk parent and teacher and at-risk child and teacher. This has been the consequence of two main trends: mass black urbanization (bringing impoverishment and socio-cultural decay) and strategies of mechanistic black-to-white integration such as bussing. We must now begin to comprehend the forces of black community disintegration and find ways to re-integrate pupil with teacher, parent with pupil and teacher with parent, toward a new black mindset.

Chapter 3

The White Liberal/Moderate Chokehold

In the re-integration of the black mindset, one major problem is that black people are not permitted autonomy. White middle class interests, definitions and values are generally antithetical to black inner city development. Yet, the white middle class (the functionary and managerial class) both in their corporate, public roles as well as in their political endeavors and reform activities, exercise an inadvertent and largely unconscious chokehold on black reform. This white chokehold extends beyond a simple reluctance to allow black people to make their own mistakes. Blacks are not allowed independence of judgment and administration in the outset.

If blacks were to move (or somebody white or black were to move) to make the kinds of transformations necessary to solve the educational crisis of the inner cities, they would have to stand against these outside and often alien white liberal/moderate middle class forces in order to do so.

First (as in the New York City conflict of 1968), they would have to fight the white-dominated teachers unions. The American Civil Liberties Union, despite its important work, also has been an obstacle to discipline in the schools and even curfew efforts after school, fighting for white adult civil liberties in the educational arena of black school children. Beyond this, in 1990, they decided to begin open advocacy, starting with abortion issues in Guam, and, somewhere along the way, will inevitably come into conflict with black interests in a new and additional sense. In fact, the American Civil Liberties Union as we have known it may have just placed a noose around its own neck. Where they once defended the liber ties of others, they now are moving to define — and thus to limit and proscribe — the liberties of others. Social services departments have joined them in their opposition to discipline, — under the guise of child abuse protection and foster care — but that is the subject of another book shortly to be published.

Before black people can solve the black educational problem — or any other major social problem, for that matter — they must in the process break free of the white liberal/moderate mainstream grip. This white philosophical straitjacket creates an absentee sovereignty over black cultural and social change.

It would appear as if white liberals and black leaders as a group believe that black people are in fact pseudo-whites — or, at the very least, that they must become white (necessarily pseudo) if they are ever to become full human beings, or "equal" to [same as] whites — that is to say in effect, white. Both concur in the requirement that blacks cannot be accepted unless they become carbon copies of whites, pseudo copies — for they can never be, and shouldn't have to be, white originals.

Yet, the persistent and insistent demand of white society is to teach blacks to be something other than what they are — white — to mimic what they cannot resemble. Blacks become whites in blackface, white people entrapped in black bodies. On the one hand, whites have created an impoverished and rejected group they nam-ed "Negroes," stripped of their true identity, their self-worth and

16

self-direction. At the same time, in the process, they have created an elite of African-Americans neurotically transfixed in the image of white people.

The new black attitude must increasingly be that we won't try to run the white schools, if whites won't run ours. Moreover, we will not tell them how to improve theirs if they won't tell us how to improve ours. Only in this way can we move to break the white liberal stranglehold and push for black sociological and psychological independence, for cultural and personal autonomy.

We must begin to participate in the definition, design and development of social policy and social agendas beyond endorsement of white liberal approaches or/and demands for simple racial inclusion and acceptance.

The Illusion of Integration

The movement for integration in the public schools came in on the wings of empiricism in social science — in this instance, the famous 1940's doll study by black psychologist Kenneth Clark. Clark's artificial laboratory finding of deep feelings of inferiority in black children was exploited to claim inherent inequality in separate black education, failing to distinguish between *separate* and *segregated* education and their contrasting psychological sequelae.

In 1954, the U.S. Supreme Court decreed desegregation in public schools "with all deliberate speed." In response to the slow pace of desegregation came the diabolical strategy of bussing. Since black children were disproportionately bussed to white schools outside their neighborhood, bussing compounded the disintegration of the education of black children wrought in the consolidation and closing of schools and the firing, rejection and disqualification of black teachers in droves.

With segregation, someone sets you apart for reasons that stigmatize and reject you. With separation, you move away from others, for your own reasons and your own freedoms. The one may be inherently inferior, but the other may kindle feelings of superiority.

With oppressed and oppressor in the same classroom, whose values, whose interests, whose needs will hold sway? These are among the inherent problems of integrated education that have continued to be hidden or denied since the late 1950's when black and nonwhite peoples in America, Africa and the world escalated their resistance to colonialism and white supremacy. These dilemmas were compounded as "desegregation" became "integration" and integration in turn disintegration of black schools, black institutions and black communities.

The Supreme Court decree of course came one year after then President Truman saw the handwriting on the wall for a segregated military at recurrent war with non-white peoples. The Korean war then being fought was producing unprecedented rates of defection by "brainwashed" American soldiers. Integration would serve the twin functions of economic consolidation and political homogenization.

The Birth of Great White Fathers:
Studies in Frankencense and Myrrh

Dangling the Carrot. Though they may seem honorable on the surface, we must guard against carrot-danglers such as white millionaires in Brooklyn or Louisiana who suggest that black children only need to know that their college tuition will be paid. While hope is a crucial ingredient in sustaining ambition, to assure college tuition (without changing much else) will have an effect not much different from free high school education, which is already assured. Children nevertheless too often fail or/and are impelled to drop out.

This brings to mind a situation in the spring of 1969, when a bitter five-month student strike of historic intensity came to an end at San Francisco State. Among the student demands was that ''any black student wishing so be admitted to San Francisco State.'' The administration settled for admitting five hundred black students. Then came the black strike leaders' hardest fight: finding five hundred additional black students at one time to enroll at San Francisco State under the so-called EOP program of open admissions and need-based financial aid.

Without really mobilizing the black child, these white millionaires place the ball in the black child's hands, throwing money to get them to do what other children better motivated do without pay. If the children are motivated, there is no need to pay them. If they are not motivated, paying may do them no good.

We must beware of frankencense and myrrh, even that brought by black persons hawking a particular experiment or school or teacher that has been successful. If you look closely enough, you can usually find a hidden reason why they are uniquely successful. What we need is some more total change, some collective approach, one not requiring teachers to be supernatural or superinnovative, or administrators who carry baseball bats to lean on, or teachers presenting imposing personal dispositions, or plans which work for middlesized, middle class white towns with relatively small black populations that lack the social decay and disintegration of the big city ghetto.

19

When things aren't working in our time, "responsible" experts tend to call for more money or resources to do what they are already doing in a bigger way. Today, socialized gambling in the form of multi-million dollar lotteries is invoked to save the schools while the schools continue to fail their mission.

We seem to forget what Plato learned from the ancient Africans in Egyptland: education is the best method of reforming both the character of the individual and the state (or society). In our time, we are hung up on the character of the individual. We see problems that are collective and immediately turn to individual solutions. We use techniques to correct the individual and culling devices to categorize him or her into syndromes such as "at risk." These collectivized expectations in turn impact upon the behavior of those categorized, who seem unable wholly to resist internalizing the expectations of their mentors and "superiors".

Teachers, for instance, come with notions that impoverished black children will not be able to learn. Many times, they bring instruments ("readiness" and "achievement" tests) to guide them in their operation, to gauge or measure their notions of pathology. Once the degree of pathology is measured (formally or/and informally), it is entered into an indelible and eternal record that follows the child throughout his days in school and long after his departure.

These are compounded in later adult life by a system of ascription called "references" and by tests on jobs where products of inner city schools may be working at a high level as a gardener or skilled or semiskilled laborer of whatever variety but may lose their jobs or miss their promotions because they cannot score highly on tests of vocational aptitude or even sociability and "personality profiles" such as the MMPI (Minnesota Multiphasic Personality Inventory).

Even I.Q. tests, now well known to be culturally and racially biased against black individuals from impoverished backgounds, continue to loom like a gun to the heads of black children (despite a groundbreaking lawsuit, the so-called "Jimmy P" case, won by the Association of Black Psychologists, in California). I.Q. test scores, averaging as many as twenty points below the true intelligence level of the black individual, are used both to help track black students (or entrap them in educational tracks) and to cement low teacher expectations of black students who then are placed in "special programs" that further hog-tie their ensuing intellectual efforts. Moreover, black changemakers in turn are impelled to dissipate their energies in vain efforts to correct these problems.

This issue came up one night in the fall of 1975, when a group of black psychologists had met at the Berkeley Marina to plan a two-day workshop devoted to finding alternatives to the I.Q. test. Someone in the group had a grant of $40,000 for that purpose.

At one point in the deliberations, the black psychologists began to recall and bounce around studies of factors affecting black children's I.Q. test performance. It was a mini-festival of competitive intellectual exhibitionism.

Finally, one of the authors who was present there remarked that, "if all this information is known about what makes a black child perform on I.Q. tests the way they do, why isn't that information given to black parents and black teachers, so that the black children's I.Q. tests could be raised? Then the white folks would find an alternative to the I.Q. tests for you."

Although the impact of "labeling" can itself be exaggerated (as in the 1970's strong-black-family resistance to "pathology" in the family), the effects of labeling black children as "mentally retarded," "slow learner," and "educationally disadvantaged" have been well documented. Culturally and racially biased I.Q., "achievement" and "readiness" tests (which test black children on things they have never been taught) can literally terrify black children. Especially when they are administered by alien forces such as middle class teachers and authority figures in adult life. This terrorism may be compounded by white teachers who come in car pools from the suburbs, speaking and dressing and walking and thinking as persons from another planet or another world — which, as a matter of fact, they are.

The "scores" in this academic game too many black children must lose are in turn used to parcel out opportunities in a white middle class defined and dominated cultural milieu.

The challenge before us may be in fact how to reclaim and package what people such as former president Harry Truman, novelists Richard Wright, James Baldwin, and Ralph Ellison, a host of jazz musicians, boxing promoter Don King, and prizewinning motivational speaker Les Brown learned before they dropped out of school. When writers who go through school don't write better, and some of the best athletes and entertainers are left in city streets by the academic farm-team system; when the unschooled adolescent grassroots culture of rapping and breakdancing and gangs continues to transform and lead cultural change—and prizewinning experts and authorities such as Congresswoman Eleanor Holmes Norton and enumerable academicians and scholars such as distinguished historian John Hope Franklin will openly boast that they "don't know the answer" to the current black condition — something is wrong somewhere.

In the clinical situation, we have seen black children whose I.Q.s were later placed at the genius or "very superior" level initially labeled mentally retarded by teachers and informal circles of adult evaluators. We have watched black boys with recognized and proven records of academic excellence in early grades fall into academic failure, then delinquency, then crime and imprisonment.

First they drop out psychologically, then drift into absenteeism and "hanging out," whereupon they become entrapped in the treadmill of petty crime and delinquency. This process is often aided by a policy of suspending or expelling students in the absence of the means to discipline them.

One day the principal of an alternative school called up. He indicated that a boy we knew to be at heart a nice and brilliant kid was in his office. As the principal showed off his knowledge of psychological jargon, the more he talked the more it appeared that the boy had been trying to get suspended for the day, through a strategy of escalation.

A week later, the boy came into the clinic and was asked if that had been true. He immediately said yes, that he and a friend at another school (also a 12-year-old) would sometimes plan to get put out of school so they could meet in the park and smoke pot.

The Passing of School Boards and Superintendents

One problem standing between the black community and educational hegemony is that schoolboard members, in many places, are not required to emanate from the community of citizens served, let alone predominant minorities or inner city pockets of poor blacks. In turn, the schoolboard will choose the superintendent — and fire the superintendent, if the superintendent takes a notion to try to really be a superintendent or to do something not already being done and not approved by the schoolboard.

In effect, admitting that they don't know how to choose a good superintendent, schoolboards will often pay thousands of school system dollars, and rely on a white headhunting firm from another town, to pick out and rate candidates for the superintendency. These "headhunters" may receive from $25,000 to $50,000 to do this. Generally, candidates are selected from the pool of superintendents elsewhere, in smaller towns than the hiring board's, or other safe candidates who are not regarded as likely to "rock the boat."

This was said to be the case, for instance, when a black superintendent of St. Louis was being "looked at" by the San Francisco School Board. He was highly touted in the news at the time for innovative and productive work in the St. Louis system. White board members (and some blacks) reportedly feared not only his political affiliations with local blacks but also the fact that he might do something different, something they hadn't invented.

We know that the schoolboard tends not to be selected by the black community, though black political bosses may exercise a broker's hand in the matter. Nor do we expect that the black community will soon control the hiring of top school administrators, though they should try. In any case, once superintendents are hired, the black community must ensure that they do their job in a way to give black children satisfaction, although it is also necessary to keep in mind that the choice of persons in ostensible authority is not the major issue. It is important, and it can be a part of the solution, just as it is a part of the problem. But more important is the system and the policies and agendas in which these adminstrators will operate — that is, what are they hired to do, what are the limits on what they can do, and who will decide these matters?

The black community also must remember that there are always at least two systems, the formal and the informal. Where the black community cannot control the formal system, the black community should be sure to generate and control an informal system.

Temptations of Vouchers: Hidden Deregulation

Black people are caught in the middle of a fight between two white tribes or factions (liberals and conservatives). An old African proverb teaches that "it's the grass that suffers when two elephants fight."

White conservatives gained ascendancy in the 1970's and continue on the rise, in part because of the ineptitude and insensitivity of the white liberal-moderate establishment, which by 1970 had seized the reform initiative from the "black power" (black consciousness) movement of the late 1960s. Although liberals are fond of harping on cutbacks of social programs and so forth by conservative administrations, the damage to the black race (particularly the destruction of the pivotal black family) was in fact due more to the ideology and agendas of the white liberals and the liberal-moderate ideological mainstream.

If the African-American race or community is going to survive, let alone thrive, it must break the white liberal grip without succumbing to or unnecessarily aiding or abetting the white conservative forces.

Black school reform, or school reform from a black perspective, must show the way to whites. In doing so, we might save not only black education but also, if only inadvertently white public education itself. The longer black public education continues to corrode under the control of white liberal and liberal-moderate direction, the more the conservative white appetite for deregulation of public schools will increase.

Unfortunately, the privatization of public school education will at best have the effect that deregulation had on the airline industry or that which the resistance to socialized medicine or even national health insurance has had on medical care.

On the one hand, we know that public school education has failed. Sadly, the possibility of correcting it in the foreseeable future now seems dim, in part because it will be blocked by white liberals and conservatives alike. For instance, as we have already suggested, white teachers unions and white teachers and administrators already in place will zealously guard their positions and their control. Then there are such groups as the American Civil Liberties Union (despite its good and necessary qualities) that have now taken up false counter-productive advocacy on social issues. For one thing, they would block any effort to seriously discipline black children in the schools. In terms of prerequisite and collateral parental discipline, the so-called child protective agencies and departments of social services will stand in the way.

Nevertheless, as we proceed to wrench black education from the choking control of the white liberal-moderate establishment, we must not walk in blindfolded or allow ourselves to be seduced by openly harsher white conservatives. We will refuse to accept a choice between the lesser of two white evils. We will turn loose the white liberal shirt/skirt tails, no longer willing to be dragged down the drain in the course of helping the white liberal establishment to save itself from itself, its own follies, and the fearsome fury of white conservatives.

On the other hand, we must be on guard against the emerging privatization of education, under the auspices or support of corporations and corporate foundations, lest we simply change horses in the middle of the stream or, worse, jump out of the skillet into the fire, trading one oppression for another less benign. The best we can hope for in the de-socialization or privatization of schools is the kind of effect that deregulation (called "decentralization" in the Chicago system, "vouchers" in Milwaukee and elsewhere) had.

White corporations can help, and black corporations should help, but neither can lead or dominate the transformation. Aside from corporate preoccupation with profit and the production of skilled workers, inner city black parents are isolated and alienated from them. In fact, black inner city parents may be more alienated and isolated from corporations than from schools and teachers.

Similarly, aside from extracurricular and sometimes delinquent use of school playground basketball courts, inner-city children are alienated from the schools. Vandalism and destruction of school buildings continue to explode on a regular basis.

Churches may constitute the only remaining positive and established institutional structures in the black community, for all practical purposes, that are owned and operated by seriously autonomous black people. Churches are the ostensibly positive places where black people are most impelled, inclined, and called upon to frequent.

We must therefore have as many school functions and school-related meetings as possible there. Churches must finally be compelled to take up Rev. King's admonition to reach beyond saving black souls to saving society; for it is in this precept that Dr. King coincides with Marcus Garvey and Malcolm X and Elijah Muhammad and all the black nationalist ideologists and black liberation theologists.

Chapter 4

An Epitaph for Black Studies

It is popular for black intellectuals these days to speak of an "afrocentric" worldview or learning style. This is good, insofar as it goes, and it is an apt way of connoting what the late 1960s black studies movement meant in speaking of "black culture" and "a black perspective" as factors in the child's learning.

It is also popular to view history as therapeutic, as we did in the late 1960s. What is missing from the afrocentric viewpoint today is a focus on "relevance." If anything, its salient claim is that African-American children experience difficulty in learning in a eurocentric context beyond what Asians might — or even Africans from the continent.

In the late 1960s, black studies had two instruments for making a course black. One was the *historical* (weaving black and nonwhite contributions to civilization and to the specific subject matter into the course content). From this the student could gain a sense of self-importance and acceptance, involvement identity and hope. The other instrument was *relevance* (tying the content and methods of the course to the daily lives of the students and stressing the importance of serving the black community and its needs — uplift and liberation). This was hypothesized to give students a sense of belonging, of commitment and purpose. Hence the importance of the *community component.*

Each course would be connected to a community practicum. Each student would be apprenticed to an expert, businessperson, or practitioner in the subject matter (which, in today's language, would now be called a mentor-tutor; at that time a mere apprenticeship).

Even a course in history would have community outreach and development components. For instance, students would be required to put on panel discussions for smaller children in church basements or wherever.

The idea was to give education back to the people, to transmit what is learned back to the community, to transfrom the community so that the community, previously excluded from education, is made more relevant to education at the same time as education is made more relevant to the community. The slogan at San Francisco State, where the 1960s black studies movement as such appeared to have been pioneered (though students and a small band of teachers at places such as Merritt College and Howard University had initially sought to do essentially the same thing without giving it the name "black studies"), the slogan was to "wed the academy and the street." At Howard, in a brief uprising in the winter and spring of 1967, in response to a U.S.-Office of-Education-directed administrative plan to make Howard "60 percent white by 1970" (announced in September of 1966), the rallying cry was "to overturn the Negro college with white innards and to raise in its place a black community relevant to the black community and its needs."

Each history class also would be obliged to start a history

club, so that over time the black community would be filled with history clubs, raising consciousness there and smashing dependency on the white university for this important affective (self) knowledge. Another course might have the class project devoted to starting an African club. In that way, instead of middle class black intellectuals paying thousands of dollars each year for trips to Africa to bring back slides of the pyramids and whatnot, Africa would be brought to the black community.

By now we might have grown to feel comfortable in calling ourselves simply "Africans," instead of "pan-Africans" or the cumbersome "African-Americans." Nobody else has to say "American" in referring to themselves (neither Italians nor Germans nor Chinese nor Asians nor Filipinos nor anybody but us), and we shouldn't have to either. We will never feel psychologically whole until we are able to call ourselves Africans. To call Africans in America "blacks" is like calling Asians in America "yellows."

In addition to such collective requirements and projects and apprenticeships, all courses would require students to tutor smaller students. This not only would have cognitive benefits for the tutored students; the black college students would provide role models (then called "flight models") in their relationship and admiration for a college student they otherwise might not meet. The student tutor would discover no greater learning device than teaching someone else.

Instead, as Harold Cruse and Maulana Karenga have suggested, black studies became topheavy with a museum-styled study or other-worldly preoccupation with Africa. Out of the ashes of the black studies movement, we again must stress the community component. The community component, with its built-in consciousness-raising, would have fueled the black independent school movement. Black studies students could have helped as staff volunteers, as

31

recruiters of pupils and financial support for the school. Now, instead of a wobbly independent black school movement, we would have a vibrant movement sending armies of black students to colleges to serve as carrier groups for other black students. They would be ready and willing and able to populate black studies courses, in contrast to the current enrollment crisis in which professors will go so far as to walk up and down registration lines begging students to take black studies courses.

Part II

The Lure

Chapter 5

Popular Misconceptions and Half-Measures

Before we can solve black educational problems, or understand the Hare Plan — or any other idea of solving black educational problems, for that matter — we first have to understand what is not the solution, particularly that which is taken for granted in conventional wisdom, or what passes for expertise today. Once we have appreciated the limitations and liabilities of the most vaunted solutions, we will be in a position to move on to correct and complete solutions that work. Not that popular beliefs about the black educational crisis have no merit; it is just that their merit is either insufficient, distorted, misunderstood, or exaggerated into falsehood.

Some such platitudes are outright myths. Others may be a necessary portion of any solution but sufficient for none. Yet they are frequently taken as the end-all and be-all of black intellectual belief and practice in America and the Western world, in turn the world at large, through the influence of multi-national media, the influence of the United Nations, university training of Third World elites in Western and westernized institutions, and governmental and nongovernmental interests groups such as the World Bank and Planned Parenthood International.

Consider for a moment, then, the pros and cons, the good and the bad, the right and the wrong, the efficacies and the follies, of the various solutions to black child and educational development now popularly hyped and heralded by black intellectuals or/and the white liberal-moderate mainstream.

Self-esteem. When people speak of self-esteem, sometimes they unknowingly have different and contradictory things in mind. For instance, are they referring to *psychological* (personal or individual) self-esteem or *sociological* self-esteem (for the race or the group)?

If they mean individual self-esteem, then what about the fact that some black children perform well in school in compensation for a feeling of low individual self-esteem? Such children may study harder to win approval from adults or to excel where peers with dispositions of self-confidence and superiority do poorly (precisely because they spend their time being popular and sociable and dancing away the hours individuals with low self-esteem spend studying).

The classical example is the bespectacled bookworm in thick bifocals or the shy but brilliant and studious wallflower. The fact that in too many inner city classrooms the naughty child quite often attracts the admiration of his peers for his very mischief, rebellion and bravado serves to fuel an unfortunate anti-intellectual ideal among impoverished black adolescent and latency children.

On the other hand, if the advocate of self-esteem means *racial* self-esteem (and they usually are not only referring to racial self-esteem but, more precisely, to esteem for the race), then where is their evidence that children who are imbued with nationalism do better academically than children of ultra-assimilation or the black bourgeoisie. Indeed, those of us who advocate on racial grounds that children be suffused with pride and consciousness of race must wrestle with the dilemma that — at least in the short run — such a child is taking on a special struggle for life in a crossover-minded, white-dominated society.

Understand us, we are not saying that self-esteem can play no part in a child's performance, or that black children do not suffer special pangs of individual *and* racial self-esteem. We are merely saying what is usually ignored, denied or left unsaid: that self-esteem is too much exaggerated as a panacea, or even a necessary ingredient to high-level academic performance among blacks. Also, we must neither confuse a problem in personal self-esteem with a problem in racial self-esteem nor restrict ourselves to personal self-esteem alone in dealing with the underlying problems of racial self-esteem. In other words, individual psychology has limited feasibility as a sociological solution.

Focusing on individual self-esteem calls on us to spend our time building self-esteem, in whatever variety or dimension, while our children's dropout and flunkout rates continue to skyrocket. We might better devote ourselves to teaching black children to do better in school, and demanding that they do so. An elevation of their performance and prestige in school in turn would generate self-esteem in them. It may in fact be easier to teach a child to read and study than to increase his self-esteem. In any case, by our present approach, we may well wind up with a lot of conceited semi-literates looking down on academic "squares," strutting around secure in the notion that "ignorance is bliss," if not oblivion.

Role-models. Echoing a suggestion we made in the final chapter of *Crisis in Black Sexual Politics* — but with his own notions and observations — black syndicated columnist William Raspberry recently wrote of the platitude of role models. Quite independent of us, Raspberry also had recently taken to asking persons who stand up spouting about "role models" as a prerequisite for high achieve-

37

ment among black youth to name their own role models. Raspberry quickly corroborated our own discovery that respondents for the most part had none, or at least were unable to think of any momentarily. In the few cases in which they name anybody, contrary to the practice of trotting out stars and eminents, role models remembered tend to be someone they encountered in their daily childhood lives. Rich and famous models either were not emulated or were adopted after the child had decided on a preference for the career the hero epitomized.

This is not to say that there is no place for heroes, or that an admired adult across the street or in the classroom cannot become a source of emulation and a model of success for a child. It is simply that our children are declining to mimic, let alone match, the heroes, stars and eminents they already have.

The role model of one of the authors was Sugar Ray Robinson; but when his mother and his principal collaborated to cart him off to college, essentially kidnapping him from his play one night, he had been given enough of a sense of obedience and devotion to the imperative of hard work and achievement to feel that, though he didn't plan to stay in college to graduation, he should nevertheless do well while he was there.

This was not so much something God-given as something that came from doing what college professors call "burning the midnight oil." His motivation grew out of the discipline and sense of obedience and deportment given him by his parents. True, his principal was well-respected and admired, but his influence on the boy (who had no wish to emulate him in any way) was more in the role or capacity of a mentor and manipulator, not a role model. For his part, the principal, though wishing the best for the boy, was acting as much as anything to obtain a tutor-roommate for his academically deficient son who was enrolling in college simultaneously. The principal and the very uneducated single mother were not so much role *models* as *dispensers* of a role to the student. Score another point for discipline and stop kidding ourselves.

It is fine to have a role model, but what we need above all is a *success role* for children — and ourselves — with or without a role model.

A role model without a success role is like a castrated stallion facing a herd of wild mares, inspired and excited, but without internal motivation sufficient to actualize, manifest or consummate the magnitude of his inspiration.

The role-model hype, which constantly wails that we as African-Americans don't have enough role models, apparently would have us wait until we have enough role models to succeed in school. But we must first have those who would succeed in school before we can have sufficient and proper role models. Otherwise, we're like the tiger trying to find his way by clinging to his tail.

For another thing, when we do endeavor to expose schoolchildren to role models, we usually seek to bring in the famous, the stars, the athletes and entertainers, when it might be better for children to emulate somebody more readily within their reach. The fantastic and the famous may be role *images* but in fact not readily translated into role *models* in the minds of the lowly, untalented and unathletic child.

Adding insult to injury, we have the nerve to turn around and discourage black children from going into sports and entertainment. Which brings us to another social deception.

If Fewer Blacks Would Take Up Athletics, Blacks Would Excel in Academe. Around the late 1960's, when blacks began to dominate professional and college athletic teams, black intellectuals began to call for black people to withdraw from sports on grounds that the athletic focus was hampering the academic accomplishments of the race. Ignored was black intellectual impotence in the face of black children flunking and dropping out who couldn't play any ball.

Meanwhile, cases of black athletes who did poorly in their course work or couldn't even read were trotted out as testimony to the horrors of athletics. Among them was a former all-American basketball player who, in his postcollege days, enrolled in Marva Collin's Westside Academy in Chicago. From that vantage point, he would go on television, backed by hosannas and shrieks from black intellectuals, blaming his former college basketball coach for the fact that he couldn't read. He should have known how to read long before he arrived at the college gates. For instance, how did he get out of middle school? Or high school? In fact, if his reading teachers had done their jobs as well as his coach, he might have become an all-American reader as well as an all-American basketball player.

In 1978, one of the authors was keynote luncheon speaker for the National Conference of Black Studies as they were drumming up to boycott athletics. At one point, as the professors pumped up their anti-athletic fever, the speaker asked them why they didn't boycott the university, since they are more oppressed than the athletes. There wasn't a millionaire in the house — and not more than twenty with tenure!

Leaders of this folly are fond of pointing out the small percentage of athletes who make it to the top. Few black persons make it to the top in any field. As a matter of fact they do better in sports than any other field besides entertainment (indeed, the justification

40

for the outcry in the first place, is their singular dominance there). Besides, former athletes not only become coaches and counselors and principals and administrators; they also are prominent among corporate salesmen, school principals and corporate middle managers, not to mention middle school and secondary school coaches. The children and descendants of athletes often have a better break, if not from their affluence, then inevitably from the fact that many of these athletes would never have seen the inside of a college were it not for athletics. Athletics surely rate right at the top of the reasons and means by which low income blacks have gone to college.

However, the anti-athletic viewpoint just happened to coincide with a desire on the part of the white race and white promoters to whiten the athletic pool. By pushing black anti-athletics and its advocates, and raising the scores and academic requirements such as Propositions 42 and 48, and early drug testing of athletes before there was even the thought of testing airline pilots, surgeons and airtraffic controllers, white keepers of the status quo were trying to decrease the number of black players able to enter sports to make room for white hopes. In pushing anti-athleticism, black intellectuals were once more serving the interests of the white race — in the name of black uplift. These intellectuals then get grants to study the failure of other segments of society and to seek explanations for black failure alternative to their own opportunism and naivete.

If black children (who watch twice as much television as white children) would turn off the television and study, they could excel in athletics and academics both — even without being Paul Robersons. In any case, it is the duty of the black intellectual first to solve the educational problems of black children who don't play any ball. Curiously, black intellectuals do not have the same animosity against the far less wholesome fields of music and entertainment (which, being more subjective than athletics, permits white people

41

to retain a more respectable place). Many of these middle-aged and senior-citizen black intellectuals are enthusiastic fans of rap and even rapt admirers and promoters of the breakdancing they dared not try themselves. Could it be that more black intellectuals can sing and dance than play athletics?

If black intellectuals had not wised up somewhat recently — and started advocating the long overdue notion that black persons who outshine white people on the playing field might also do well as coaches and managers — we might have thrown out the baby with the dishwater. We might have halted our sports dominance but, in this deneutered condition, continued to flunk and drop out of school.

Stereotypes, Myths, the Black Image, Labeling and Deficit Theory. Those who advocate or exaggerate the importance of this category of factors tend to be preoccupied with getting the white race to recognize black worth. Philosophers have known for centuries that what trips up the slave is the desire to gain recognition from the master. We keep trying to persuade white people to recognize and acknowledge our worth as a people. We keep trying to impress the wrong person when we need to impress ourselves.

If you thought you could clearly outrun somebody else, you'd gladly give them a slight headstart, say, "take twenty yards — I'll catch you." If you thought you could beat up somebody in boxing gloves, you might offer to fight them with one hand, tie one hand behind your back. But if you're not certain of your superiority, you try to get the advantage as the white man does.

42

Indeed, social historians have advocated that racism, or the ideology of racism, originated in fear, when Europeans (in whose minds darkness called out the terror of night and the symbolism of the negative, the macabre, solemnity, dignity and death) were driven by the mother of necessity to cross the uncharted seas in giant sea monsters called ships. When they came suddenly face-to-face with masses of jet black persons, they were petrified, their fingers were frozen to the triggers. Their predatory, reactive impulses to dominance in short time were undergirded and cemented by the ideology of racism.

Before the 1960s black power movement, with its black-is-beautiful and pride-in-Africa orientations, you could get a rise out of the average black person by so much as suggesting that blacks were better athletes or dancers than whites. People all said the idea of black superiority in athletic endeavors or dancing was a vicious stereotype.

As late as the early 1970s, one of us was quoted in *Jet's* "Words of the Week," saying that blacks shouldn't apologize any longer for our excellence in any area of life, including sex (a popular black intellectual preoccupation at the time was extolling the mythical quality of the idea of black sexual superiority). The quotation concluded that, although "there are psychosociocultural forces behind it, the fact remains that black males excel in athletics and black males excel in dancing, and sex is a form of both athletics *and* dancing."

Stereotypes and myths, like other paratruths such as jokes, legends, and witticisms, are based on a certain reality which they merely exaggerate into the ludicrous but do not invent. The conventional wisdom is that we must correct the black image in white people's minds — especially white teachers — before we can perform better, when the reverse might just as well be the case, if not more so.

Black leaders judge books and movies and television programs by the simple yardstick of their perspective on the black image, unmindful of whose interests they are otherwise serving. For instance, books might project a "positive" black image but otherwise promote an anti-black or white sociopolitical agenda just as books might portray a negative image of blacks but indict white society for the predicament under scrutiny and simultaneously push for or justify a black alternative or remedial agenda.

In the realm of education, this translates into a proscriptive belief that we must present black people only in our positive features in order to motivate black children to learn. When we were growing up as black children, before all the "positive" black intellectual enlightenment of today, we were regularly told by our parents and teachers that, precisely because we were black, we wouldn't get half a chance and that we therefore would have to study and work twice as hard as whites did knowing we had to be twice as good as whites to gain an equal footing.

The black intellectual hordes advocating the singular and pretentious presentation of the positive fall into the strategy designed by Erik Erikson, who in turn was led by the sociologist Talcot Parsons seeking to tone down the black movement of the 1960s. They fail to see the conservative essence of the fact that if you don't see anything wrong, you won't feel impelled, other things equal, to do anything to make things right. They follow the shortsighted sociological theory of the 1970s, the theory of secondary deviance.

The theory of secondary deviance caught fire among white sociologists in the 1970s, as part of the "labeling" theory (including the "deficit theory") argument favored by black intellectuals' suggesting that if you call somebody something deviant, they will begin to act that way. While this may under many circumstances be true, the fact remains that in the correction of deviant behavior (as the example of Alcoholics Anonymous, Weight Watchers, etc. would suggest) you may first need to recognize and acknowlege the deviance before you can make a concerted or prolonged effort to change it.

Cloaking the deviance in a mechanism of psychological denial or pretense leads only to inaction and futility, such as eased relentlessly into place within the black movement in the decade of the 1970s. You may understandably and correctly seek to spotlight as many virtues and strengths as you can, but you ignore your weaknesses and your errors at your peril, leaving them to fester.

Accordingly, black protest in our time continues to revolve essentially around an acute, if not pathetic, desire for racial acceptance, limiting itself to: 1) civil rights protests for acceptance or a portion of whatever the white liberal-moderate wing of the powers-that-be may define as desirable; and 2) the search for bygone ancient African glories.

While the quest for civil rights is necessary, it is not sufficient. Moreover, civil rights quests can easily be misconceived (as in the case of "integration" and its strategy of bussing, which quickly replaced "desegregation" as the panacea for black educational attainment in the late 1950s and early 1960s).

In the singleminded search for bygone ancestral glories, we are left with our heads buried in the ancient Egyptian sands. Bogged down in the past, we neglect to generate or utilize any new sense of pastness as a springboard to a new and collective future. We fail to define the new society or new social agendas for the world. Thus, black leaders and intellectuals take no stand on the major issues of the day, other than belatedly to echo white liberals, in whatever arena.

Afrocentric vs. Eurocentric Learning Styles. We are locked in an ideological straitjacket. We openly and unashamedly clamor for simple white acceptance, like a drowning man, latching onto a crippling preoccupation with rationalizing our failures. This is not to suggest a single retreat, not one backward step, from the task of piling blame on white racism, rather to take care nevertheless to balance ourselves and our quests more firmly and appropriately upon the tightrope running between responsibility and blame. It is a counterproductive, one-eyed vision that focuses on one without the other — to blame white society without retaining responsibility and self-initiative for blacks or to give responsibility to blacks without blaming white society, without placing part of the blame and part of the responsibility on both.

The notion has arisen in our time that it is mainly a difference in culture or learning styles that restrain black achievement in the lower classes — learning styles centered in Africa, "afrocentric" (called "a black perspective" in the late 1960s black consciousness movement) as over against those centering in Europe, "eurocentric"). As a matter of fact, it may even be slanderous — as we suggested in *Crisis in Black Sexual Politics* — to suggest that black children, unlike Asian and others, can only grasp cognitive knowledge through one cultural learning style — no matter which one that may be.

Though children understandably would be expected to experience greater ease of learning in their familiar culture, this is only a part of the problem and can be exaggerated, and is. Indeed, the value of the late 1960s black studies emphasis on black culture and community lay more in its powers of student motivation to learn and commitment to community service and change than in concessions to black incapacities, rationalizing them, or defending the black image. Not understanding this, present-day black studies faculties and administrators readily permitted the renaming and removal of courses in black math and black science to remedial sections and divisions outside black studies itself.

In any case, the properly motivated and mobilized black child can learn, as we shall see, in Greek or Latin or any other course content or cognitive realm, as Marva Collins, armed with a personal gift for connecting to her previously rejected and discarded students, would appear to have demonstrated in Chicago. However, we are searching for a collective strategy, one that does not depend on rarely gifted teachers or students, but on whatever we (or for that matter any society anywhere) might be able to devise or muster en masse.

The Hare Plan does not rely on dilletantes or exceptional individuals, rather on mobilizing the genius and capacity of the group or race as it finds itself in negotiation with the world. Meanwhile, we must understand that *it is not the content of a course, or some experimental change in the content of a curriculum, that will solve the black educational crisis.*

Understand that in the late 1960s the need to center ourselves in Africa and all things African — cultural styles in particular — was recognized as a racial right and even a collective necessity, but only in the sense that a left jab is necessary to the prizefighter's armamentarium. It was, is, necessary but not sufficient. Like the left jab, it properly appears at the beginning and even the end of an arsenal of blows, but culture was never meant to be the end-all or be-all for African freedom and elevation in America any more than for Africans on the continent; and it never will. The predatory, genocidal character of white society continues apace to cripple the continent of Africa — afrocentric cultural learning styles and all, customs, traditions, rituals, dashikis and all.

47

We have taken a very good thing, our African cultural legacy, and stretched it like an elongated rubber band into a tenuous and crippling incapacity. There is in this no claim that African-Americans as a group identify too much with Africa or the afrocentric. We would be among the first to recognize and complain that we do not identify enough with Africa — and we were. We are saying on the contrary that a part of the reason Africans in America have not come around to identifying with Africa or/and the African legacy (especially following so promising a beginning as the late 1960s black consciousness movement) is related to the fact that those who advocate the African connection or the afrocentric ideal have stretched it so thinly in the presence of no other strategy that many black individuals see readily through its overdrawn potential.

Early in 1971, one of us warned in an editorial in *The Black Scholar,* ("Wherever We Are") that the "otherworldly" approach black intellectuals had begun to take toward pan-Africanism was becoming an alternative to struggle here and now. It was the beginning of what Edgar Ridley, in *The Neurological Misadventure of Primordial Man,* lambasts as our inclination to place symbol over substance, or status over substance, as E. Franklin Frazier witnessed while living and teaching among the *Black Bourgeoisie.*

Black History as the Dominant Solution. This category includes both the idea that knowledge of black history alone is essentially enough to transform black students into high academic achievers as well as the overemphasis on history born of the notion that knowing our history is about all we need to know to set us free. True, we should know our history for many, many reasons. But if knowing your history alone could set you free, then historians would be the freest persons of all, at least freer than physicists, engineers or mathematicians. The global, magical power and pedagogical value of black history are only slightly less tenable than the emerging lionization of "multicultural education" and a "global curriculum" suggesting that what ails us is white people haven't been taught our history.

Many adherents of the multicultural movement (including those of a card-carrying nationalist bent) will stand up and bemoan the European rape of ancient African culture while studiously and relentlessly assimilating to the most drastic cultural destruction that the race has ever experienced — that which has brought on the black family devastation and the thwarted socialization of black children today.

Female-Headed Households and the Romanticizing of Black Single Mothers. In the early 1970s, a speaker seeking to cry out about the rise of single black mothers would be chastised and accused of suggesting that "something's wrong with being a single parent," that women should have a choice to be single. The speaker would reply that there may not be anything wrong with being a single mother, that a person must make the best of the situation in which she finds herself, but that there is something wrong about the fact that a black woman is more likely to be a single mother because of what somebody else, some other race, is doing to black men. Also, there is something wrong with adapting and accommodating to that situation, romanticizing single parenthood rather than rising up to change it. Besides which, you cannot say that it is a "choice" to be single, when it is not something the single women prefer; such a choice must be called by some other name.

By the mid-1980s, when the rate of black single mothers had doubled, the black intellectuals turned right around and joined white opinion makers suggesting that our main problem as a race is that we have too many single mothers. In reality, the negative consequences of single parenting on black educational achievement rests more on the factors producing the both of them than on the situation of single parenting itself. These factors include of course those of poverty and sociocultural oppression. Although what's hard for two may certainly not be easy for one, let alone childrearing to a single mother, children can learn and achieve in an impoverished single family if other factors are present or available — as we shall see.

Welfare. Many people continue to believe that welfare is the major problem, though only a minority of black inner-city black children are on longterm or chronic social welfare. This is not to say that welfare does not have a negative effect on the psyche of the race, particularly in the way it is designed and operated, but welfare was with us long before the contemporary downturn in black educational performance and, therefore, cannot be used to explain it or the catastrophic black family breakdown and the disintegration of the socialization of black children that erupted around 1970, just as a constant cannot be used to explain a change. There must be some new quantitative or qualitative intervention.

Impervious to this, solutions held out to rectify the problem of black socioeconomic stagnation among black and African peoples on the continent and in the diaspora [for instance, "workfare" (before it was discouraged by defensive labor unions) and "women's development" as promoted by such white-designed and dominated organizations as World Bank and the United Nations] will prove to be counterproductive at best and in all probability will compound the problem of family and social instability. If too many black women are on welfare because they are single mothers, in turn because there is a shortage of viable men, then to educate and develop black women singularly while failing to elevate black men will only increase the number of women without suitable males, even if it doesn't increase the number of men without a viable mental attitude or psychosocial will. This in fact already has been exactly the black result of the unilateral, unisexual white feminist movement of the decade of the 1970s.

Teenage Pregnancy. Although the teenage pregancy hype (sold to black intellectuals in the mid-1980s at a time when black teenage pregnancy had been on a steady decline for twenty years) now appears to be waning, it continues to thrive amid the condom-in-the-schools agenda discussed elsewhere in these pages.

Studies show that black teenage mothers are about as likely to have already dropped out of school at least a year before they get pregnant. Pregnancy is only one of the reasons they drop out of school — not to mention why they don't resume school after pregnancy.

Because it is possible to say that the major delinquency of ghetto girls — unwed births — is directly attributable to the influence of some male, much time is now being spent in an uncertain attempt to teach black boys "male responsibility" for protecting girls against pregnancy, rather than urging them to marry, as once was fashionable and backed up by the shotgun.

In many ways, "the black male" is increasingly the scapegoat. We believe that black males, like black females, are not inferior beings, that they are generally living out the behavioral scripts of their social and psychological experiences. We must change the circumstantial scripts or/and the social stage to change the behavior.

If, as we believe, black males are not biologically inferior, then we must look for sociological reasons for their failures as a group. To imply that black females are naturally superior to black males is to impugn the heredity of black females as well, indeed the black race itself, as producers of inferior males. To suggest that black males can solve their problem by merely trying harder is to ignore sociological forces and to imply that the demise of the black male — predicted by us relentlessly since 1969, despite white society's conspirary of silence since 1969 — is due to the insufficiency of the black males's own efforts. Although we undoubtedly were among the first in our generation to advocate that black males try harder, it is nevertheless necessary to explain why they have not tried harder, or why in trying they have continued to fail their roles to the dissatisfaction of society and their women and children.

The Black Male and the Black Male Child. It is increasingly popular, now that the horse is out of the barn door, for black intellectuals as well as the white media and others who refused to deal with the black male during the past twenty years currently to cross over and cry about "the endangered black male" and to launch programs and experiments aiming to correct the black male, or some portion of black manhood.

These include black intellectuals who wailed throughout the decade of the 1970s and beyond against "pathology" and "deficit" theories in their mistaken tendency to treat black male failure essentially as a psychological phenomenon. They collaborated with white society to place black males on a backburner from 1969 to 1985 and indeed suggested to black men that it was sexist to be conspicuously masculine or even to give expression to the idea of male/female differences. Once black men had relinquished the masculine imperative, these experts and authorities turned around and began to ask, with the white media "why aren't black males being men?"

All-Black Male Schools. A potentially controversial approach now being advocated around the country, beginning in Milwaukee, Chicago, New York City and, abortively, in Tulsa, Oklahoma, is the so-called all-black male immersion school. Black males would be placed in all-black male schools (or, to skirt legal obstacles, predominantly or explicitly black male schools) and "immersed" in history, culture, values and socialization deemed appropriate to the black male. While some school boards and critics have feared "separatism" and resisted these schools on conventional rainbow (integrationist or assimilationist) grounds, others (including white educational administrators) have enthusiastically endorsed them attesting perhaps to the delicate nature and potential misuse of the idea.

Modeled after all-male military and parochial schools, coupled with conventional black studies teaching of knowledge of self and culture (with a nod to the idea of black male-specific cultural learning styles popularized by Janice-Hale Benson and Asa Hilliard), and the "mentoring" concept associated with the contemporary rites of passage movement, such schools could at least be as useful as all-male white military and parochial schools. However, great care must be taken to avoid stigmatization and the possibility that the schools will become merely remedial dumping grounds for troublesome black male pupils or pernicious pretexts for resegregation.

In any case, the all-black male immersion schools do not address the problem of educating black girls — other than to imply alternative all-black female schools. There will also be the insinuation that black boys uniquely can learn only in race-sex-specific groups.

Perhaps this situation merits at least an examination by black educators and white boards of education of the Nation of Islam's educational model which not only anticipates the positive elements of the male-immersion schools but also incorporates females in a context providing sufficient psychological and pedagogical distinctions along gender lines within an otherwise multi-gender terrain.

Meanwhile, surely the male immersion schools, properly handled, can be a means of solving the black male educational problem, but obviously not male-immersion schools alone.

The all-black male immersion school, for good or ill, reflects the lastditch level of black frustration with white-dominated mainstream school systems and a search, by whatever means, of political and psychological independence from white control. The techniques they propose are perhaps more symbolic than utilitarian.

The Ujamaa (Swahili for ''family'') school in the city of New York, proposes to have a special emphasis on Hispanic and African-American males, specifically the history, achievements and problems of the particular ethnic groups. This amounts to a portion of the black studies movement of the late Sixties (minus the component of community involvement, which was to be applied to existing black schools or black sections generally, male, female or coeducational). The most useful ingredients that could come out of the all-black male school movement are the very things they may not foster — that is, the kind of discipline and ideological commitment characteristic of Nation of Islam and white male military schools.

One of the latent functions of the presence of Hispanic males, let alone white males and females, is to dampen, restrain and restrict the fervor of any black male ideological teaching. A Catholic church in Ohio was criticized recently for adding a pro-life flavor to the pledge of allegiance — ''with liberty and justice for the born and unborn." As one student explained, "we're at a Catholic school and should be expected to [uphold] the Catholic values."

Programs to expose black boys to black males can help, but they will not be sufficient for black male transformation, not to mention black females. If we aren't careful, we may soon have set in motion an irreversible trend to house black boys in separate and remedial dormitories or/and educational or residential treatment centers.

As a matter of fact, since these words were first written, the idea was suggested by the president of Howard University, in Washington, D.C., who was featured in an article by Ethel Payne, "Education for Blacks in the 21st Century," in the March, 1991 issue of *Dollars and Sense* magazine, proposing: "24-hour a day urban residential schools where children [boys and girls] at the elementary and secondary levels live in dormitories, eat, learn and sleep under supervision."

Increasingly, black children (especially black boys) already are housed in juvenile halls, residential treatment centers, reformatories and related institutions. The difference is that, in the universal institutionalization of inner city black children, the inmates would stand accused of no crime except being "at risk" — that is to say, black and poor. They would nevertheless be incarcerated by the society that oppreses them, but fails to educate them because it can not or will not take the steps necessary to do so.

There has long been a sentiment in that direction among white conservative thinkers. Charles Murray, author of *Losing Ground*, has even proposed in *Commentary* magazine (circa 1985) that dormitories be established to house black unwed teen mothers. Murray's proposal followed by more than a decade similar hypotheses referencing male and female inner-city black children on the part

55

of the eminent late University of Chicago psychoanalyst Bruno Bettleheim in his report of his study of the kibbutzim in rural and small town sections of Isreal, *Children of the Dream.*

What we must always be on guard to know is whether a strategy grows out of the spirit of a people (in this case, black people), or is it one sold to us or forced upon us by the white opinion-makers and powers-that-be. This is not only true of barrack-style or pre-concentration camp type solutions, but of any other plan. For instance, bussing (the strategy of integration taken to its logical, or illogical, conclusion) was not invented by blacks but accepted by blacks after the NAACP was persuaded to embrace it. Then we go another quarter of a century in bussing or barracks before experience teaches us what we should already have known.

Integration. Inspired by the white liberal-moderate establishment and the 1954 Supreme Court decision that separate education is by definition inferior, many black intellectuals continue to believe that the ultimate solution is but black-to-white integration, as against black elevation by whatever means or by contrast white-to-black integration (considering that Rome defeated Greece but Greece conquered Rome). Elijah Muhammad, founder and messenger of the Nation of Islam, explained at least as early as 1962 that there's a difference between separation and segregation. Segregation exists when somebody sets you apart for characteristics they deem to be inferior. Separation is the act of moving away or seeking independence of mind or space yourself, for your own reasons at your own time. There is a crucial psychological difference between the two which is too often missed.

In 1963, one of us wrote in a *Negro Digest* article, "The Negro's Escape from Freedom," that integration and separation are promising means to the ends of elevation and empowerment, but, like any other means, they tend to lose their effectiveness when they become full ends in themselves. While the first tends toward conscious and unconscious accommodation, if not absorption; the second may amount to nothing more than unconscious avoidance. It will be an irony of recorded history (we went on to say in the 1963 article), that whites used segregation to hold us down in the first half of the century and integration to hold us down in the second half. We had not even anticipated the "crossover" imperative that reigns supreme in today's "rainbow" era.

Multicultural Education: The Mirage of a Rainbow Imperative. Currently there is emerging a movement toward "multicultural education," which will have the latent or unintended consequence of a deceptive co-optation of black or race-specific studies.

Piggybacking on an expressed white administrative desire (though little known or heard beyond the campuses, except for an overall "crossover" imperative for blacks in the realm of popular culture) to foster "cross-fertilization" of black studies with traditional disciplines, this movement includes a trend to step-up official offerings of alternative black studies courses (particularly for white students) in traditional academic departments.

Supported by naive and shortsighted black studies advocates, multicultural education openly fosters the teaching of black and ethnic history and culture to white students. Not only will this serve to water down the original black studies thrust (which was geared to black or race-specific education and community change), we cannot afford to teach all white students black studies, when black studies programs already go wanting and hurting for lack of financial support. Moreover, it is based on the false assumption that white domination and racism are due to cognitive ignorance. We also know from much experience that the white-controlled and dominated system will only permit that black history that is palatable to white students (the *Roots* variety), with the nonviolent Rev. King as its epitome and model militant. What is emerging under the aegis of "multicultural education" is not black studies but polka dot studies.

Meanwhile white feminist programs (whose directors often sit on black studies hiring committees but not vice versa) flourish in relative affluence to black studies and frequently raid black studies programs for black female instructors. Yet, nationally prominent black studies black male scholars, revered and popular lecturers, with well regarded and seminal books to their credit, plus proven records as superior professors before they were fired or/and went to jail in the fight for black studies programs, will be unable to get fulltime (not to mention tenured) positions even in black studies departments. When chosen or preferred by handpicked black studies recruiters and committees, these brilliant scholars will be blocked by white overseers, often aided by black feminist collaborators.

However, some of these black studies black militant casualties have recently been able to gain employment in black studies programs by assimilating to a white liberal ideology or agenda, particularly unisexual anti-natal feminism. Aside from the routine machinations of emerging thought control, this is nothing more than the crossover imperative transplanted from the bookstore and the bandstand to the classroom.

In regards to both afrocentrism and multicultural education, it is true that black inner-city education needs to be culture-based, but it also must once again become family-based and community-based, just as it is city, state and nation-based now — increasingly, world-based. But, above all, black education must be race-based in the interests and agendas it serves as well as culture-based.

For us, "nation" has a twofold meaning: 1) nation as country and 2) nation as race (or "nation within a nation"). We recognize that there are other factors such as class, that where there is classicism there must be class struggle, just as where there is racism there must be race struggle. But for us as African-Americans, race is the quality that cuts through everything else in our oppression. Black educational failure is a race-based problem and, therefore, one way or another, must have a race-based solution.

In addition to "multicultural education," there is a fad now to focus on changing the curriculum. There is possibly good in that, but not that alone. Once a child is motivated and impelled to study and learn, he or she can learn any curriculum.

There may surely be some good to be derived from righteous changes in a white-dominated curriculum — for instance, studying black history (as we advocated in the late 1960s) — but more benefit will come from consciousness of present-day black realities and mastery of the wherewithal to deal with them.

More benefit will be derived from changing other facets of the educational milieu, not to mention the socio-educational milieu (beyond the focus on ego-educational or individual psychological dynamics so popular today). For instance, contrary to all the talk about "quality education" and raising standards, we should bear in mind that, when all is said and done, it really does not require a master's degree to teach first grade children how to read.

In fact, there is an inverse statistical correlation over the years between the number of years of school completed (or the number of courses in teaching methods) and the educational performance of inner city children. As the education of teachers has increased, the educational performance of the children has worsened. The contemporary raising of test scores and degree requirements and related credentialing not only has been ineffective and counterproductive; it has tended to be racist in its consequences, however unintended, leading to frightened predictions of a drastically whiter teaching profession in the years ahead, even in the inner city, where most of the students will be black. If you think you have a war zone now, you haven't seen anything yet.

To teach white people black and other cultures, aside from not being cost-effective and duplicating introductory anthropology courses, makes the same error made by early 1960s efforts to "win white hearts and souls." It assumes that if white people knew better they would behave better. But the Civil Rights Act of 1964, outlawing segregation in public facilities, saved us from a decade or more of futile entreaty.

Echoing this sentiment, in a speech delivered at the 1990 American Federation of Teachers conference, Rutger's (Camden campus) University professor Robert J. Cottrol warned:

"Unhappily, multicultural education has only a marginal ability [to achieve its stated purposes]. The students most at risk — those from decaying inner city neighborhoods, those from broken families, those who join gangs in fear of their lives, those who are the heirs of a culture of despair that has developed in all too many of our ghettoes in the last generation — will not be inspired nor have their lives radically changed by the addition of a multicultural dimension to their educations, however much we might hope so. The addition of black, or Hispanic, or Asian, or Indian heroes and role models might inspire a few such students, but multicultural education cannot be seen as a remedy for society's neglect of its cities, the poor people that dwell in them, and the urban schools that will shape the next generation of Americans.''

Corporate Control. Schools are increasingly being co-opted ("adopted") by private corporations. In Miami Beach, Florida, the school board even hired a private company to take over the selection and training of the teachers (who presumably were already trained by the universities) and the designing of the curriculum. The company proposes to use the same techniques in Miami slum schools as they use in the affluent suburbs of Pheonix, Arizona. The teachers union even agreed to waive aspects of its contract with the district so that the sample school can pursue its plans to hire first-year University of Miami graduates to work as part-time teachers. Of course few such grad student teachers will be black or Hispanic, in contrast to the transient student population.

This bright idea cropped up after the superintendent of schools ran ads in national newspapers and magazines for ideas on how to run overcrowded inner-city schools. In other instances, school boards frequently pay headhunting firms from $20,000 to $50,000 to find a superintendent, suggesting they don't even know how to choose a superintendent, at least how to find one, let alone how to run the schools. Although any opposition is faint or unheard, the budding corporate school-takeover movement is considerably more threatening than school privatization.

Decentralization and Deregulation. On the one hand, we do well to question centralization of authority in the hands of a few — usually white or whitepicked — hands. In a sense, then, just about any transfer of authority from absentee school boards to domestic communities and parents is commendable.

The idea of parents electing their representatives and participating intimately in the managerial affairs of schools (including hiring and firing principals, shaping curricula and binding budgets) is a welcome one. Never mind that the Chicago program of structural decentralization was struck down as unconstitutional by the Illinois Supreme Court, whose questions concerned the "mechanics" instead of the intent of the decentralizaton scheme. We are reminded once again that we will have to expect to do battle with constituted white authority in terms of both mechanics and intent before we can truly educate black children.

However, the Chicago example may also suggest that we will have to avoid the temptation of expending excessive energy fighting battles that will yield limited results even if won. It is not that the choice of occupants of seats of educational authority, day-to-day decisionmakers, is of no special moment; only that the rules, polices and values that guide them are more important. If parents or/and citizens are pulled into programs of "school-based management," to help manage what school boards are already doing, little of lasting value is likely to occur. It becomes a war of musical chairs, a seesaw of symbol and substance.

We must also bear in mind that, while we fight for equal representation and participation in institutionalized or formal structures of authority and management, we must build informal structures outside constituted authority in order to wield much power.

For instance, in the way that prison gangs may control prison yards impervious to formalized prison authority, black people at the grassroots level can create committees and groupings guided by what black Wisconsin State Representative Polly Williams calls going from "the bottom-up theory as opposed to the top-down where bureaucrats decide what they want for low income families". However, blacks must have an impact not only on the choice of teachers, principals, schoolboards and superintendents, but on what these persons can implement.

Wisconsin State Representative Polly Williams created a firestorm when she persuaded Milwaukee governing bodies to establish a limited voucher program in which almost a thousand low income families could qualify for approximately $6,000 per child to spend on private non-sectarian schools in the city. Despite the bawling by white and black liberals fearing the dismantling of public schools, Representative Williams made the compelling point to the Los Angeles *Times* that "the system is not doing its job, [and] we can't keep funding the failure we are funding."

To charges that she is being "used by conservative whites," Williams replies: "it doesn't matter if conservative racists and bigots have the same idea [as she has]." When critics cry that voucher plans "reject public schools rather than changing them," they certainly have a point, but they fail to understand that rejecting public schools may be the necessary first step in the process of changing them and their relentless contribution to the "poverty industry."

Her "choice" plan is at least a beginning, though no cure-all; we must tread carefully and be on guard that privatization of education does not become or represent a form of deregulation in the public schools equivalent to deregulation in the airline industry. Given her characteristic initiative and spunk, it is not likely that Representative Williams will lose sight of the twin goals of overhauling public school education as well as providing a general model for private schools so that students with vouchers will have something of value to choose.

At the same time, we must view with suspicion a proposal in Oregon to allow parents tax credits toward the cost of a child's tuition, as a parent must have the income or/and the property to take or obtain the tax credit. Like tax breaks increasingly given as fertility incentives, this would be class-biased. However, we should welcome the competition between advocates of privatization and socialized school reform — and, from where black people sit, may the best plan win.

Sex Education. Sex education is now required (without parental consent) from kindergarten through high school in such cities as New York, which can only undermine further the already quickly-waning parental authority. This parent-child schism is especially likely to be damaged when parents disagree with the school's program and point of view on sex and the child knows it. Increasingly, schools that are failing to teach children reading or basic academics are electing instead to solve problems outside their bailiwick — teenage pregnancy, health problems, child abuse.

Dropout Rates. This begs the question. Why are black children dropping out? Why do they too often fail while they are in school? Even when dropping-out does not follow poor grades, it may be merely another way of failing, just as failing may be a product of psychologically dropping out or withdrawing from school requirements though remaining in school.

Teen Unemployment. This cry went up in the mid-1980s coincidental to a decline in the number of teens available at a time when there was a proportionate increase in the number of jobs needed to be filled in fast food chains. If anything, a working teen may find his study habits disrupted or cramped, and he or she risks assimilating to out-of-school and unschooled working peers, in the process growing accustomed to cars, fine clothes and the routine rewards of a regular salary.

What the average teenager needs is not so much a job as a parent with a job, nay, two parents with jobs these days, if you can get them. The teenager working for less may contrarily usurp a job from somebody's father. In fact, the only thing that put a dent in this hype (as in the case also of the workfare agenda) was fears of a cheapening of labor and wages overall.

Teacher Attitudes and Expectations. Like the other popular misconceptions, the notion that attitudes and expectations of teachers affect a child's performance contains more than a modicum of truth. However, the black educational problem cannot be solved by merely changing teacher attitudes and expectations, even if we could significantly change them *a priori*. As a matter of fact, if we could manage to seriously raise white teacher expectations of black children, as things now stand, we would probably face newly escalating rates of black flunking, as the inner city children continued to fail, for whatever multiplicity of reasons, to live up to the new white teacher expectations.

Lack of Motivation. Nobody can tenably deny that black children are motivated to desire and seek socioeconomic success. At the same time, black children exhibit no difficulty creating and learning barbed rap lyrics and the dazzling intricacies of social dancing, slick slang and street smarts. Our challenge is to steer that motivation toward socially-acceptable or institutionalized channels in a society that limits black opportunities to fulfill these motivations.

In rejecting the goals and means that reject them, black children may be adapting as best they can to the situation in which they find themselves. This may be what sociologists have in mind when they bemoan the enthusiasm with which black underclass children are motivated to adapt to street values and the "black adolescent subculture."

Money. Money counts, but no amount of money can solve the black educational problem using presentday practices. More and more money has been spent already — with fewer and fewer results. More money is surely useful, but not money alone; money is not the answer and money is not enough.

Curriculum. The problem of curriculum and (curricular change) is discussed more fully elsewhere in this volume. What students study is not so much the issue as how they study it and for what. Not that curriculum plays no part, but with more and more curricular changes, our problems have worsened. Indeed, one of the main reasons black studies has not worked up to now is that administrators and professors who followed the black-led campus rebellions of 1968-69 misconstrued black studies to mean mainly a change of curriculum or a change of course content to "black" without essentially changing anything else.

With the activation and unleashing of such strategies and forces as the Hare Plan, students will be able to study almost anything, except as it may be distorted by contemporary or future occupational and social needs and the new demands of society or the marketplace itself. Even then, graduates would be able to quickly acquire anything they need which they weren't taught in school. Without the kinds of ingredients suggested by the Hare Plan, no amount of curricular change will ever be enough.

Teacher and Staff Development. This is mainly a money-grabber for persons with programs and projects. Again, this is not to say that staff development is not important, just that it is not enough and also that it all depends on development for what. For the past several decades, to our knowledge, teachers have known that staff development was little more than a joke; and they continue to see it as a means mainly of getting out of the classroom. They long to escape the classroom, and they appear instinctively to realize that there is a limit to what they can do inside the classroom. If the teachers long to get out of the classroom, imagine how the students feel.

Dress Code. Already there is a move afoot to implement dress codes and uniforms or facsimiles — from Florida to Oklahoma and across to California. In an Oakland (California) black elementary school, children are asked to wear clothes of particular colors: boys, blue pants and white shirts; girls, blue skirts and white blouses. Girls skirts come from a uniform supplier, seen as one more means of cutting down the clothes craze that has children robbing and even killing each other over designer footwear and jackets, at the very least to erase the Bloods/Crips brand of blue/red warfare.

Teacher advocates of the code also hope it will calm classroom jealousy, disruption, distractions and strife fanned by children mocking each other about the clothes they wear. Additionally, the dress code proposes to cut down on class conflict ("you can't tell the rich from the poor," the chairperson of the school's parent involvement committee explained). Further, the dress codes are designed to diminish the sometimes agonizing effects of television advertisements and clothing commercials on poor black children's minds.

Although in the Oakland school, as well as likeminded Northern California places, the code is voluntary and tentative (because current regulations do not allow the children to be required to wear uniforms), in a recent Oklahoma City experiment, the board of education has been considering the establishment of a task force to study the use of mandatory dress codes to counter gang symbolism, fads and paraphernalia. However, the board was leaning, as of this writing, toward such strategies as prohibiting excessive jewelry, drug paraphernalia and obscene or provocative dress rather than decreeing uniform standards outright.

The task force may learn what parochial and private schools have known traditionally: beyond the benefits already mentioned, uniforms not only make it easier for students to concentrate on studying; they also facilitate a frame of mind conducive to discipline, obedience and receptivity to the goals of the group enterprise, the school or classroom. The psychological effects of uniforms and uniformity in the rehabilitation of the mind so characteristic of groups such as the military, asylums, rehabilitative and corrective institutions, as well as parochial schools and the Boy Scouts, have long been noted by sociologists such as Erving Goffman.

The Spanking Taboo. With the advent of ultra-permissive childrearing, spanking (which had served the human species very well for many millennia) suddenly became taboo. It came to be called by the sinister name of "corporal punishment" — first in the schools, then in the home. Poor black children, for whom the peer group and the environment are anti-social, were left without sufficient reinforcements to proper deportment and positive social conduct, making it more difficult for them to gain a clear core to their personality. This situation is today supported by official regulation in twenty states, plus thousands of local schoolboards in other states. The claim is that violence breeds violence; yet violence (including "excessive" compensatory violence on the part of parents, teachers and caretakers) is more of a problem today than ever before and ominously continues to multiply itself.

An Epilogue to Misconceptions. Although we have pointed out limitations of the foregoing "popular misconceptions" — we conclude and concur with the advice Mao Tse-Tung gave to W.E.B. DuBois and his second wife, Shirley Graham, when they visited him in the People's Republic of China. As Mrs. DuBois related to us on a visit to America sponsored in part by *The Black Scholar*, Mao was profuse in his praise of DuBois who, in modesty, kept confessing that he had make a lot of mistakes. Mao told DuBois that the only mistake an oppressed race can really make is to do nothing at all to oppose oppression. Anything else is merely a part of the process of ironing out or eliminating the spurious solutions in order ultimately to arrive at the correct solutions.

Chapter 6

Final Reflections on the Idea of a Plan

We have probed among the problems of the public schools in search of a deeper understanding, to arrive at the necessary solutions, and we hope that we have described the situation and its resolution not as others, or even we, might wish things to be, but essentially as they are, or must become, one way or another, in the not too distant future.

In any case, nothing much that is now in place appears to be sufficient. This leaves everybody, to some extent, somehow a part of the problem.

It is against this backdrop that we offer a plan which will involve parents, mobilize community, lighten the worklife and workload of teachers, spice schoolfare and spark student learning.

We will tell how the educational performance of underclass black children — especially young black boys, whose educational malady is most acute — can be elevated to an appropriately higher plane.

We intend to put no one out of a job, but on the contrary,

to offer a last chance, lastditch plan for public school personnel to save their jobs — before there is a mass black inner city exodus from the public schools that will make the white/black middle class private school movement pale by comparison, one equal to or greater than the disorganized and self-defeating passive-aggressive black inner city exodus now known as "dropping out."

We are laying out one last hope, one final alternative, to the emerging possibility that black youths, reminiscent of the drug gangs today, will move toward a still more total control of the socialization, initiation and education of themselves and other ghetto youth.

We recognize that what we are proposing is an ideal situation and that no particular person or school or district or system will employ the plan in its entirety. We hope all will seek to implement at least a part of it. Some of our suggestions — as a matter of fact — are already being tried by a number of innovative individuals and systems (e.g. Chicago, Portland, Milwaukee, Kansas City, Los Angeles, St. Louis, New Orleans and New York City). We wish only to augment and to codify their contributions into one big fist of educational change, to spread the good word to others, and to enlarge the support and reinforcement of these brave and unsung pioneers. Others will build on our approach and theirs, improving it as they may. For all of these, we hope to act as a catalyst.

Many are giving up on the very possibility of educating black children in the existing public schools. If the situation continues as it is today, may our plan help them in their courageous move to secede from a decadent academic order.

Although many educators and activists will dare to employ the approach we are calling "The Hare Plan," we are aware that some will not. They will choose instead to spend their days wondering why they were left behind. We are writing for people who want to change the schools, improve them, not those who, out of fear and timidity, racism or whatever excuse or advantage, want to cling to the status quo. There will always be those who are satisfied with whatever exists, even a status quo of decay and devastation. They prefer, for whatever reason, to keep it that way.

Our plan by contrast is to prevent further corrosion of the education of black children and, in the process, to halt the relentless and tragic trend toward higher and higher dropout rates and the heavy drift of black children into delinquency, self-destruction and incarceration.

Currently, everybody is caught up in an endless scramble for new and more dazzling teaching techniques and tactics, when we already have too many techniques, far more than we need. With more and more techniques, if anything, we appear to have less and less understanding.

However, not only do existing techniques, flawed as they may be, work well enough for other races; these techniques are also relatively effective for the middle class within the black race. But, although class, or poverty, is connected to the issues we are addressing, we are confronted with a particular kind of breakdown and escalating divergence in a social order and the impact of these forces resulting in educational failure.

We continue to recognize the collective or societal sources of the problem, but stubbornly concentrate instead on techniques and experiments, plans and proposals, for dealing with or correcting *individual* casualties or children "at risk" of becoming casualties to our social dilemmas.

We fail to see that the problem is more *outside* the classroom than within it and there (outside the classroom) also will be its resolution. Solutions will hinge more on what is done outside the classroom than within it; and, accordingly, the teacher must either move her/his turf beyond the classroom or begin to dispatch and direct new squads of paraprofessionals remote to the classroom to do so.

Just as teachers must increasingly do their work, if not their teaching, outside the classroom; more and more persons beside the teacher must begin to teach within the classroom.

One of the most important skills of teachers in the future may be their ability to assess and utilize the talents and strengths of parents and other persons in the community. Such persons may even be used to teach or assist in teaching, especially in the summer session, when schools might more strenuously take up the function of black heritage schools and freedom schools. They would use the same buildings but different personnel, parents and paraprofessionals, staggering vacation time to fit the need. All must be culture-bearers and teachers of black culture and consciousness.

Merely to have the parents and community involved will tend to be beneficial. It isn't necessary that they teach theoretical physics. They know how to cook sweet potato pies, repair cars, sew, quilt, jitterbug, repair roofs, and whatnot. The idea is that they, that everybody, is involved in the educational process. This is, at the level of the African village, the afrocentric way: if one person learns something, everybody else will know it shortly, each one teaching one another.

By involving the parents and the community, we not only invoke the laws of imitation (including routine systematic and relentless role modeling); we start to give the child a success identity, the identity under which we have at the same time begun to mobilize the parents and the community, exploiting the things that they can do and do well as we involve them in the educational enterprise from which they have been excluded.

Returning to public performances reminiscent of once popular night-time school-closing plays at the elementary level can take the place of superfluous nursery rhymes and bring more public interest and parental involvement, as parents are more likely to come to the school if there is a performance.

We should never have eliminated spelling bees. Preachers of only a generation or two ago knew well that if they could attract the children to Sunday school, they could get their parents to church. These preachers would go out into the community during weekdays, after school, and roundup and recruit the children. Home mission societies and men's groups could aid in this regard today.

We must revive the idea of the contest in academic life, the idea of the game and of competition. In the process we might raise the idea of black academic excellence to the level of excellence in athletics, producing academic Mike Tysons and Magic Johnsons, or Michael Jacksons and Spike Lees.

Academic contests and games might begin to serve the function once served by such as bingo games and quilting parties and could be peripheral to the task of organizing children with parents, organizing parents with other parents and children with children under adult direction. To the extent that adults do not provide games and rituals and bonding and identity, to that extent will the children and adolescents provide it for themselves. The gangs are testimony to this today.

Beyond Just Saying No: What Is To Be Done?

It is not merely cognitive education of blacks — nor even their attitude toward cognitive education — that has been distorted. The distortion of the black self and of self (affective) knowledge and the place and possibilities of themselves as blacks in the world (socio-cultural) may be more acute.

Like a doctor treating an ailment, it is necessary to deal with the entire body, with the blood stream and the entire, pulsating body. All the techniques of teaching in the world that do not take account of the child's life outside school will leave but a disjointed liaison between the home and child and community and school.

Once the school has done its work from nine to three o'clock, the inner city child is impelled to retreat home by night and, under the cover of darkness, turn into the kind of character that can deal with life on mean, impoverished streets in a quixotic world. By day, he is required to crawl out of his coccoon and move out from his nocturnal transformation to compete in a game of social mobility denied but not designed for him.

We have, therefore, tended to emphasize doing things out in the world of the child, with the parents, and with other practitioners and persons in the child's real-life, non-school existence.

We also emphasize the public performance, the celebration, the ritual, the game, the contest and the spectacle beyond conventional school-based "varsity" athletics and "extracurricular" fare. We refer more to the need for community-based and race-specific activities designed to mold a new black *social parent* and the educational development of the impoverished social milieu.

In the years before integration, black schools had assemblies on a regular basis, plus we had to recite and sing every morning in the first hour of "devotion." The hour of devotion had the effect of a sedative, a hypnogogic calming of children's energies and anxieties preparatory to the academic work for which it also ritualistically prepared us.

In regular "asssemblies," principals and teachers would set forth the school's intents and expectations. This gave the children and the staff something to hold on to and something to look forward to. Assemblies provided the children, at both the individual and class levels, invaluable opportunities to perform. The singing of school songs and the black national anthem gave them imponderable pride.

Education can no longer be restricted to the school buildings and ground, even if we were in charge of what goes on there. The school itself nowadays is like a research lab, set apart from the real world and culture of the students, from life itself. At the highest levels of education, this fact is acknowledged in part by references to "the ivory tower" or, as we ourselves would sometimes say in the late 1960s, "the ebony tower." It is like a would-be swimmer of the English Channel who learns to swim in an artificial tub and practices in the swimming pool but never goes into the channel or any wide and choppy waters. The Comer Model of the Yale Child Center, backed by the Rockefeller Foundation, has been most prominent in promoting parental involvement. As early as the 1938 White House Conference on Children, it has been known that the parent was the first and most continual teacher. Yet parents have been alienated and almost pushed out of the educational process.

Along with urbanization and related factors which alienated parents and teachers (including the usurpation of parental functions by the educational institution and the use of teachers *in loco parentis* by parents themselves, an active tendency arose on the part of teachers, strapped with increasingly larger classes, to discourage parental participation such as excessive tutoring of the child at home. Such children moving ahead of the class might be disruptive to group learning, it was felt.

Add to this the fact that many parents today were born in the 1960s (a period of tremendous social change). Increasingly, they will have been born in the 1970s (a period which promoted the independence of mothers from family obligations and commitments). Even if they were born in the 1940s or 1950s, they came to adulthood in the 1960s or by contrast the 1970s-80s decades of apathy and technocratization.

From the 1950s onward, in any case, they experienced permissive childrearing, reflected by the rise of the influential Dr. Spock. They would tend in turn to expose their children to ultra-permissive childrearing, which was climaxed by the child abuse protection movement which today wrenches children from parents believed unable to care for them or properly parent them, for whatever reason, real or imagined.

In a sense, this policy of parental usurpation had long been followed during the emergence of formal schools. Now is the time to return education to the world of the children and, insofar as is possible, to the parents and other copartners in the educational process.

Protests by African-Americans and Indians already are mounting against white adoption of black foster children as well as a push to favor the natural or biological parents. A parallel movement should readily be apparent for the schooling of black children, to halt the white usurpation of the control and diurnal possession of black school children.

There are basically only two main approaches to correcting the black child's performance: 1) motivation of the individual child (or socialization, which incorporates motivation) and 2) mobilization of the black community collectively toward the reclamation of the control and initiation of the new wave of black child mobilization.

To do this, we must first recognize that teaching techniques and mastery of new techniques — let alone existing techniques — will never alone do the job. We must cease wasting time and effort on the technical illusion.

The public school correction will not be attained by concentrating on the individual child, especially children who are already lost, already casualties of our urban social decay. We know that sentimentality and crocodile tears will flow over that statement while we let fleeting droves of reachable children and others yet unborn go relentlessly down the neglected and uncorrected tide. We must motivate and mobilize entire groups and collectivities of children as well as persons affecting them.

We have suggested that teachers and educators will solve the problem in what they do outside the classroom — indeed outside the school — more than inside the classroom. To do so, they may need collateral personnel, new go-betweens, new mediators, and even security workers, persons preoccupied with black social outreach, dedicated to connecting others to the inner-city child and the child to other social and cultural niches from which he or she is now excluded.

We may need to turn away from speaking of the classroom to the idea of the *classworld*. By "classworld," we mean not only the world of the classroom itself; nor even the fact that the classroom is merely a replica, a microcosm, of the student's larger existence;

we aim to stress that the classroom is a very small portion of the child's learning environment.

It is true that we must have changes in the curriculum, but changes in the curriculum will not be enough. Indeed, it appears that the more the curriculum has been changed, the more things have remained the same, or even deteriorated, in terms of test scores and performance. Even black studies would no doubt be more effective today, if we who were among its architects in the late 1960's could have prevented the simplistic substitution of black content in a new curriculum called "black studies." What we needed and wanted was a new approach to scholarship and pedagogy. The new methodology and ideology envisioned in the late 1960's movement — even without much changing the curriculum or course content or even the titles of the courses — would have been far more effective.

Technomania: Methods and Madness, Tyranny and Titillation

Nor do solutions appear to rest in merely "raising standards" when existing standards are not met, or calling for money for things that money cannot buy, or funny-puddy techniques in crazy-quilt brainstorming approaches.

Educational reformers today tend to focus on instructional methods. They use buzzwords such as "quality education" (more recently, "multicultural education"), "smaller classrooms, more money, longer school hours for students, shorter hours for teachers, curricular recasting, floating teachers, an extended schoolyear, an extended schoolday, stricter teaching credentials, ad infinitum. None of these has solved the problems.

Many call for more in-service teacher training, bilingual education, black studies, or even black history. Teachers say that parents don't want to learn, while parents and teachers say that teachers don't want to teach.

Scholars and social critics speak of pathology in individual student psyches, poor self esteem, the paucity of black role models (which at best places the cart before the horse), and parental alienation.

Not that many of these are not part of the tangle; they just aren't as powerful or deterministric as their advocates claim. Besides, they tend to address themselves to the doctoring of the indivdual pupil and his psyche. Beyond that they direct appeals and entreaties to individual parents, pupils and teachers alike to try harder, mistaken-ly believing that massive individual persuasion can transform the educational realm and the social order that generates and sustains it.

The teaching of Black (and African) history — insofar as the two histories can be differentiated — is necessary and desirable, for many, many reasons. But history is not the panacea it is popularly believed to be. If knowing your history alone could set you free, historians would be the freest people of all. Historians are no freer than mathematician, lawyers or physicians, and history is not the only road to consciousness. Sometimes it is no road to consciousness at all, can even become an alternative to consciousness as in the twilight of the "black power" movement.

In our plan, we are building on the late 1960's black studies community component we helped to design. The Comer Yale University model seeks to involve the parents. We wish to involve the community. We also want to change the culture of poverty and to teach the parents to teach the community as well as the children.

Beyond this, we piggyback and build on the community component black studies initially had. We believe that psychological solutions to sociolgical problems are prone to be curative and remedial. We have stressed the sociological solution.

Aside from changing society or/and the world of the inner city child — at least culturally, if not socioeconomically — we mean to include in the "sociological" such strategies of collective motivation as the community component, the rites of passage movement, the NAACP's ACT-SO concept, the Urban Leagues mentoring program, Simba-style boys clubs, and so on.

Just as teachers must increasingly do their work, if not their teaching, outside the classroom; more and more persons beside the teacher must begin to teach within the classroom.

One of the most important skills of teachers in the future may be their ability to assess and utilize the talents and strengths of parents and other persons in the community. Such persons may even be used to teach or assist in teaching, especially in the summer session, when schools might more strenuously take up the function of black heritage schools and freedom schools. They would use the same buildings but different personnel, parents and paraprofessionals, staggering vacation time to fit the need. All must be culture-bearers and teachers of black culture and consciousness.

A piecemeal, fractionalized approach to educational development and change will not be enough, any more than in the case of a doctor attending to various symptoms without taking the blood pressure or otherwise treating the entire system. It follows that no amount of innovation in what is done in the school from 9 to 3 will be enough.

Even holistic approaches to schools that neglect parents and other agents and forces of socialization will prove insufficient. Focusing on *cognitive education* (acquisition of skills, information and knowledge) will not be enough, without attention to *affective education* (knowledge of self and self-potential, who you are, what you want to become and what stands in the way of it). Attention also must be directed to the functional — how the individual can apply his knowledge toward negotiating the cultural, political and socioeconomic terrain.

We see our problems correctly as sociological or collective but, searching for solutions, we inevitably resort to the psychological realm. We immediately look for a sample of individuals to subject to some program or experiment to upgrade their individual behavior.

Meanwhile, we neglect to do anything to change the social circumstances — let alone societal processes. In educational reform, we typically endeavor to repair or transform individual schools without fundametntally altering the school system, let alone the culture of socialization external to the school.

When we take up group or collective approaches, we tend to rely on campaigns or appeals to children to do better, and be better, than they are or can be under present conditions; e.g., "just say no." The overwhelming majority of children are doing the best they can, considering their circumstances. The best results will be found in changing those circumstances and in the methodology of socialization, not simply in saying no.

Part III

The Solution

Chapter 7

The Hare Plan

This Plan may be implemented in whole or in part by any individual or group wishing so — after first reading the previous parts of this book. Individuals may be self-chosen or commissioned by some other authority. Groups may spring forth out of those already existing or they may be freely formed for whatever chosen purpose. It is possible to begin today.

Do not be too ambitious in the outset so as not to doom yourself to disappointment and discouragement by the frequently fruitless cranking to and fro that is necessary to start the rusty engines of black social change too long stilled by intransigence, doubt, division, confusion and immobility. Like getting out of the sprinter's blocks, getting started can truly be half the battle.

Start, then, where you are, with what you know. Call a friend, a few friends of a similar mindset, and tell them to call a few or many friends and acquaintances. Arrange a small get-together, with no strings attached and no necessary activity previously arranged. Your goal is to start a black think tank, consisting of a small group of friends, relatives and acquaintances to begin with, who will meet to talk, study and think about the problem at hand, the educational elevation of a people.

Merely getting together on a regular and continual basis can in time generate (or permit the generaton of) uplifting tasks and activities. If small groups of black people, of friends and neighbors, come together in a regular way, however informal, to grapple with the goal of black educational excellence, much will be learned and much can happen beyond our initial hopes or expectations. Eventually larger groups (or casual coalitions of the small groups) will emerge in natural course. We need only commitment and the will to act.

Beyond timidity and opportunism, we stand immobilized by two main tendencies: 1) we wait for some profound or magical formula (which in itself serves to confound and petrify us); and 2) whenever we get together, we tend to do so in mass-audience situations pulling for revivalistic preaching, rapping and handclapping, when what we need is dedicated and tightknit small groups that allow for more intensive individual participation and mobilization. Rather than tapping intensely what we each and severally know, we become victims of entertainment, of expressive behavior, and feel-good spectatoritis.

Waiting for imponderable and magical formulas, we are like athletes who refuse to jog or do calisthenics but sit with a rabbit foot on a neck chain appealing to supernatural and artificial means of conditioning. W.E.B. DuBois, who is credited with inventing the scientific study of racial conflict, if not modern sociology in America, finally concluded that knowledge is not enough, that people already know pretty much what it is that needs to be done, if they would only act. We are not doing what we already know. We argue over the relative merits of the strategies of DuBois, Booker T. Washington and Marcus Garvey, when in truth as a people we have never really tried either one of these approaches.

Rationale and Framework. What is the Hare Plan? The Hare Plan is a total strategy, an approach to achieving the goal of black inner-city educational excellence. It goes beyond the classroom, on the premise that the problem of black educational excellence today will not be solved by what is done in the classroom alone.

Not that what is done in the classroom does not remain important; we mean only to emphasize that we already have plenty of teaching methods and educational techniques. We have more and more techniques with less and less understanding and fewer and fewer educational successes in the inner city. We also have many good teachers whose total repertoire of services go unused or even misused. It is time for something new.

Recognizing that the solution is not in the classroom so much as outside of it, that the most significant work will be done outside the classroom rather than inside of it, that no amount of changing merely what takes place within the school building, let alone within the classroom, will satisfy our inner city educational needs, we increasingly prefer the concept class*world* to class*room*.

We must bear in mind moreover that education consists of three main categories: 1) *cognitive* (acquisition of knowledge, of information and skills), the preoccupation of education in modern and postmodern society); 2) *affective* (knowledge of self); and 3) functional or *socio-cultural* (knowledge of the social terrain or manipulation of cognitive and affective knowledge for the advancement of self, community and society). What has been neglected most starkly in the education of inner city children is the *affective* — and secondarily, the *functional* — while we narowly concentrate on the *cognitive,* predictably without success.

We must be aware that, much in the way that schools in the not so distant past came to take over or assume some of the childrearing functions of the family, we have arrived now at a time when the usurpation will run both ways. Increasingly, other institutions or agencies (religious, corporate or economic, social service departments, police, departments of public health) will assume or co-opt many functions once left to schools.

Having already recognized the importance of extra-classroom and extra-school involvement, we may go on to divide the pedagogical terrain into three basic spheres: 1) the *home* (including parental involvement); 2) the *community;* 3) *society* (including social policy, social values, agendas and social processes, including mass mobilization).

We may then proceed to apply two simple dichotomies to each of the four main spheres: (school, home, community, and society). Care must be taken to approach each sphere in two directions: 1) working from the outside inward (the *centripetal*) versus working from the inside outward (the *centrifugal*). Further, we must deal with both the *individual* and the *collective* planes.

We operate on the principle that to ignore or fail to take account of any of the foregoing facets of school reform is to restrict ourselves to unworkable piecemeal strategies. This in fact has been our practice up to now, and this has also been a major portion of our problem.

Chapter 8

The Home

The home is the castle of the parent, but the parent or/and the representative of the parent (parenteacher) must not be a stranger to the school. This is the centripetal direction of parental involvement (from the outside world into the school). The parent must no longer be a stranger to the school. In the other direction, equally as vital (the centrifugal, or inside outward), the teacher and her/his representative (the paraparent) must reach out in brave new creative ways (taking pains at the same time to do what is merely basic).

In the centripetal direction, the parent is involved on some basic level in helping to teach the child; while in the centrifugal direction, the school will implement some program or measure to assist and teach the parent.

The paraparent (to be elaborated upon shortly) has a primary duty to engineer and negotiate the education and teaching of parents. Many parents may be impelled to enter some instructional program. Some will engage in workshops provided in parenting itself. However, paraparents should help to reinforce the parents in what they are doing with their children, including helping each parent to reinforce each individual child. A pat on the back, a word of praise, a well-deserved plaque or other public recognition or symbol of a job well done, a friendly and comforting ear for routine parental expressions of frustration, can level mountains of defeatism and social lethargy. The work of the paraparent will ordinarily go a long way in creating and mobilizing parental concern for a mass psychology of black educational excellence, but the Hare Plan goes far beyond the parent *and* the paraparent, as we shall see shortly.

Meanwhile, many people fail to realize that the helping parent need not be any more knowledgeable than the child in academic terms. Indeed, the motivating parent may not necessarily transmit knowledge per se to the child. What the parent must be involved most in doing is motivating the child to study. For it is psychosocial motivation, including an attitude of hope and responsibility, that the black child must have; not any particular information, nor any particular amount of information. With proper motivation for the opportunities awaiting him or her in school and society, the ordinary child could readily acquire what an ordinary child needs to know.

One social experiment found that the school performance of children improved merely by having parents require that children review their homework assignments and their mastery of them with the parent. This worked even when the parent did not know exactly what the child was talking about.

However, we can no longer leave the job of educating black inner-city children exclusively to parents (often impoverished, single and uneducated), just as we do not leave the job of transmitting cognitive education to parents of middle class white children, but send them out to schools and nurseries. The difference is that the inner-city parent will need special help to infuse the child with the affective and functional components of education as well as, or more than, the cognitive.

We will therefore take as a primary goal the creation and promotion of the *social* parent (taking pains not to undermine the parental autonomy and authority of the biological parent in the way that social service departments now operate with parents accused of neglect or abuse).

In the evolution of social parenting, we will do well, wherever possible, to promote the return to rituals in family life toward bringing both extended and nuclear black family members back together and bonding them in the common realities of daily life which obstruct the education of our children. This should include family meals, even rituals of blessing the table, family prayers of whatever denomination, reclamation of African variations such as Kwanzaa and rites of passage and others that may be beneficial, created or derived.

This amplification of bonding — and the sanctification of comraderie and togetherness, in contrast to the contemporary practice of microwave television dinners, phonemate machines and bolted doors — will then be available as a cushion and as energy to stimulate and support black educational endeavor.

It is already acceptable to use somebody other than teachers to supplement certified classroom instruction. There are even school systems now trying to cut back on expenses and personnel by asking veteran teachers in their late forties and fifties to take early retirements in order to make room for newly hired teachers. New teachers come at a cheaper salary level and are younger and more pliable. This sets in motion the Peter Principle, causing schools to lose and miss the wisdom and experience of the veteran teachers. Simultaneously, it contributes to the transiency already likely to pervade the family and school lives of impoverished inner city children.

In this connection, we may learn from what is happening

in some California districts where bilingual migrant field workers are being recruited to bridge the transition of migrant children from rural to urban classes, giving them the extra attention they need (including that which overburdened parents cannot give), bolstering confidence in the children, embodying role models and so on. An unexpected by-product or latent function of one such program in rural California has been that many of these teacher's helpers have gone on in turn to obtain more formal education for themselves, including becoming credentialed teachers.

Not only do many black inner city children experience difficulty with the language, speech and diction of middle class teachers; they also are frequently impelled to move from neighborhood to neighborhood within a city or from rural to urban or regionally, South to North or West and, now also, North and West to South and urban to rural, one city or state or neighborhood to another. Like migrant Spanish-speaking parents, black parents also need instruction in basic academics such as reading, writing and arithmetic.

Further, in the effort to attract bilingual teachers, the Los Angeles Unified School District is proposing to permit immigrant college graduates to teach for five years while they learn English. Similarly, black adults who know black English or/and the nuances of inner city black dialect should be allowed to teach in the lower grades (where basic skills, orientation and socialization are so vital) while they proceed into or through college.

A Los Angeles spokesperson conceded to the Los Angeles *Times* that "for a while, foreign-born kids are going to have to bring their teachers with them because the reality is that we can't get enough to meet the changing demands of our students." According to the Los Angeles plan in the Hispanic or foreign-born case, the Spanish-speaking teachers will be assisted by English-speaking aides. The black bring-your-own teacher could be assisted by subject-matter specialists such as education majors preparing to become full-fledged teachers in the future.

Not only might black inner city children begin to bring their teachers with them — and some of them should be in the form of parents — even when the black child has not migrated from one town to another, or from one neighborhood to another within a city, he or she is a *psychological* and *sociological* immigrant (if not a physical or territorial immigrant) to the white-designed and dominated world of the inner city school, a world that often appears more concerned with standardization than education and with maintaining the fiction that all children under present circumstances are taught the same thing, when in fact they are not.

One of the things, additionally, that have prevented a parallel approach for black children up to now is the white determination to regard black people as "white" without rewarding them and treating them as white or making them as educated or affluent. They regard black children as different from white, but insist upon black children acting and thinking as if they were white, to do this within a white framework and a white-designed milieu. Thus the black child is presented with a maddening, diabolical and double message: never forget that you are different, but we all must forever pretend that you are the same.

Call for Black Paraparents: The Birth of the Social Parent

The very word "educare" (from which "educate" was derived) originally meant "to lead out." It is the duty of those who would be educators to do this. The etymology of "parent" by contrast is "to bring forth." The parent brings forth and the teacher leads out, though we may need to generate some hybrid worker — perhaps to be called "*parenteachers*" — to be teamed with "*paraparents.*"

Parenteachers not only would give instruction or teaching to parents in a variety of areas; they might also stand as the parent's representative at school. Among their duties would be to serve as liaison between parents and teachers, and they would be devoted to social knitting — that is to say, rebonding, reconstructing and restructuring relationships, partnerships and collaborations between and among teachers and parents and students and teachers and parents. In addition, they would provide surrogate services befitting the new *societal* parent, inasmuch as teachers and collateral school workers now have begun more openly to assume, but not take over, many functions of the parent. The deprivation is greater when there is no parent, no father, or the parent or father is failing his role. We must provide means such as the rites of passage to complement and supplement parental functions.

Additionally, we might have family or/and neighborhood and district scholastic competitions on the order of athletic marathons and decathlons, wherein collective reading scores would comprise a percentage, math scores a percentage, etc. This would not take the place of or replace varsity academics or even *academic* singles or mixed doubles. We could have academic leagues on the order of the YMCA basketball leagues and the adult bowling leagues popular in the black working class. These would provide collective reinforcement for individual rewards (including parental encouragement). At-risk parents have more time than money, so we must find ways for them to put in more time. The middle class with more money than time by contrast can begin to put in more money without waiting for outside doles, direction and control.

Activities can be organized that crisscross teaching and parenting and foster linkages and connectedness in the life of the child. This might include the development and monitoring of parent-*partner* and teacher-*partner* as well as parent-teacher programs and committees.

Rather than focus on new techniques of teaching — when we already have too many techniques to little or no avail — our task is to educate the teacher as a social being, to raise the teacher's social awareness and social proficiency.

A teacher once boasted to us that her school had received a grant to "expose children to culture." She then decided to take the underclass black children to a white ballet. While there is nothing wrong with that on the surface, the teacher seemed unaware that she passed African dance troupes and other cultural events across from and nearby her school. She marched students past group cultural events on the way to see "Swan Lake" (where the ugly duckling is black but turns into a beautiful white swan after being cleansed). She never appeared to realize that part of the "culture" her children needed exposure to was something other than that of the sixteenth century European royalty.

When confronted with all of this, she simply replied, "does that make a difference?" She could not understand that a child not only needs affective knowledge (knowledge of self); affective knowledge is frequently being given inadvertently and negatively simultaneously with cognitive knowledge.

The need to develop the social parent, however, does not erase the necessity for mobilizing more involvement on the part of individual or traditional parents themselves.

Not only is it essential to involve parents in the school and surrounding education of their children; we must find ways to resurrect, cultivate and surrogate the parenting role and function itself. This is particularly so in the case of the black male child. Such groups as the Coalition of 100 Black Men, Simba, the National Urban League's mentoring program, and the Year 2000, are among those that have done initial work along these lines. We will need far more of these, more closely aligned with school activities and personnel. Here lies a great opportunity for the so-called Greek- letter fraternities to play a major social role.

Not to slight sororities, we also need female social surrogates to supplement, collaborate with and coach black underclass single mothers. This could benefit both male and female children. In this connection, some acceptable way must also be found for black girls to interact more with male paraparents or social surrogates. Children not only need to learn to relate to the same sex parent; they also need relationships with opposite-sex parents for better adjustment to adult male/female life. We mean to include platonic and communical relationships as well as romantic or sexual relationships. Although black mothers generally are left in the home, we now have a generation of parents who themselves were victims of the continuing breakdown and usurpation of biological parenting and the black socialization process. We have single mothers who themselves were not properly parented, not properly mothered, let alone fathered. We therefore must provide the children (and the parents) with new models of mothering and fathering, at the same time taking pains not to fall into the current trend to undermine the respect, autonomy and authority of biological parents and parenting.

We must find ways to mobilize and activate black parents, to involve and heal and teach black parents, functionaries and community leaders. Do not be discouraged if at first they are reluctant to do their part. They too are victims. Through brand new bonding and group work with parents and teachers and functionaries and community leaders, we will lay the foundation for a new beginning. Once we have the ball rolling, the new orientation will become at first a fad, then a fashion, and finally will be woven into normative and institutional values.

Parental Involvement

We must find new ways to bring parents and teachers back together again, new ways to bond parents and teachers, generally and particularly. We have chosen to concentrate in this script mainly on goals and objectives, leaving you to your own initiative and inclination to come up with strategies and tactics appropriate to your own milieu, time, place and personal disposition. Not that we won't make suggestions, but in the long run it is best to find your vision in the process of acting in combat with your own reality. W.E.B. DuBois, who invented the scientific study of race relations, if not modern American sociology, finally decided that knowledge is not enough, that people already know pretty much what needs to be done, if they would only act. Instead of doing what they know, they borrow another moment of hesitation in the search for magical and grandiose push-button schemes that, in their very magnitude, discourage and stymie hope and initiative. All it may take to stop segregation by race on public vehicles is for one very ordinary woman to take a seat in the white section and refuse to get up.

In our canvass of the entire country, we find that most teachers agree that it is possible to do little without getting the parents involved. One of the most frequent complaints in our seminars and workshops is the low level or almost total lack of parental involvement in the schools. However, teachers typically continue to make the mistake of depending on the parents to come to them.

Meanwhile, many parents, not wanting to come to the school so much as to get their sick child, will go so far as to tell the teacher that the child isn't really sick. Although this may be true in many cases, it is obviously inappropriate to make such a determination, sight unseen. Others automatically jump to the child's defense in conflict with the teacher, unknowingly undermining the child's ability to respect and learn from the teachers or to learn to take responsbility for his own misdeeds instead of blaming authority figures or others.

The acute alienation and fear between parent and teacher in turn impacts upon the child. We may have to return to sending a note or a letter home on a regular daily basis. In the People' s Republic of China, small notebooks (variously called "connection books") or "communication books" are sent back and forth between parents and teachers. One of the stipulations of many Catholic schools in the United States, (and many other private schools) is that parents give a minimal amount of voluntary time as a requirement for their child's matriculation. Studies and experiments repeatedly show the importance of parental involvement.

One school produced an escalation in pupil performance by requiring that parents be continuously involved in group therapy during their child's matriculation. Another school simply required that parents daily review or check the homework of the child. It was not necessary that a parent understand the work. Merely going over their child's work routinely led to elevations in the child's performance, for reasons which could tickle the speculative capacities of a graduate psychology student. In any case, as a philosopher has said, the idea is not so much to understand the world as to change it.

Many parents have expressed the feeling that they can't be comfortable going to the schools. Teachers and the new parenteachers and paraparents will have to meet them initially in the neighborhoods and in the streets. Walking through San Francisco's Japantown, we frequently find that the streets have been fenced off for some Japanese cultural function. In the black community, this would have the added effect of slowing down a lot of the compensatory car mania and related partydown recreation and tape decks and spinning and turning of wheels which could be replaced with some less hedonistic, more productive endeavors and orientations.

100

Although our primary goal is to get parents more involved in the schools, we must first meet them where they are and teach them. To paraphrase Kwame Nkrumah, we must "go back to the people, live with them, love them, learn from them, teach them. Start with what they know. Build on what they have."

Many students do not achieve because they are children of nonachieving parents. It is not merely a parent's illiteracy, not just the inability to prime and prod their child to a higher social purpose that retards a child's performance. It is also an attitude toward education (including the habit of study) that has been distorted by poverty and oppression. This distorted attitude in turn is passed on by the parents who have little experience and no tradition with book learning and diligent study.

Parents will often travel willingly to the school for parades or Halloween parties, spending hours helping prepare the party decorations and to get the children ready; and the same is true for sixth grade graduation. We may need to put on more spectaculars and public displays toward making the school or school-oriented activities in the churches and communities enjoyable and ego-gratifying. For instance: bake sales, box suppers, cake walks, fish fries and gumbo fests, spiced with reading and rapping and breakdancing and spelling bees or whatever suits the place and the moment.

We will not only need to excite the imagination of the children; we must begin to erase the tainted residue of unpleasant experiences and negative attitudes toward schools harbored by parents and adults who will tend to pass them on to the children.

If we are to get the parents involved, we may first have to get involved with them, starting where they already congregate. Bingo games and diverse competitions between schools and churches beyond the realm of athletics alone could readily expand the scope and intensity of black academic participation.

Whatever happened to the spelling bee? Suppose the word got out that college tuition and the promise of prestige, wealth and power awaited the winners, step-by-step in organized "leagues" and the like.

We are building here on the idea we gave to the NAACP in 1975, on which they founded their ACT-SO program, except that we are proposing that it be infused more widely into the grass roots social fiber of the inner city black community, not merely something for middle class children already doing well in school to show off at annual conventions, far removed from the average ghetto child's environment. We might capture something of the participation fad of today's jogging marathons — if rewards and funmaking were multiplied.

Even if there were no scholarships promised or assured to such academic contest winners, the glory of winning could provide the hook for adult and academic mentors to persuade the child to pursue or/and be pushed into a college track. At the very least, we could begin to infuse academic activities with the kind of festivity and importance we give to athletics without knocking the athletic excellence of which we should be proud. Scorning athletics is not only futile; it seeks to throw out the dishpan with the water. If our children would cut back on the marathon hours (twice the white average) they spend watching televsion, they could have time to excel at athletics and academics better — without being Paul Robesons.

Return to the Source

Whatever happened to old-fashioned discipline? Much of the solution to the socialization (including the education) of the black child rests in merely returning to what we once knew, what served us well enough before things took the downturn in today's "progressive," "enlightened" or "modern" (now "postmodern" or "postindustrial") era. It will be necessary to return to what worked and to approximate or reflect what schools were like before dropout rates soared, before juvenile delinquency was virtually forced upon young ghetto males (when the children had a reasonable chance to be law-abiding, without being pressured and threatened and terrorized into crime, dope dealing and other mischief), before parents and teachers were alienated from each other and in turn from the children.

Discipline, including spanking (now called "corporal punishment") — stealing a phrase from the penal world, as if the child were strapped in an electric chair — once served us well, for many millennia. With the onslaught of postmodernism, the trend toward ultrapermissive childrearing escalated (for ultra-permissive childrearing was but one of the continued trends of individualization antagonistic to the family). Permissive childrearing ultimately alienates parent and child, for the child knows no authority, no fear or moral retribution, he is bound to respect.

For the middle class white child whose benign environment supports and reinforces his or her socializaton and social elevation, permissiveness may well be sufficient. For the inner city child, whose world is cramped and crowded and crazed and crippling and filled with divergent and degenerate distractions and lures, including threats to his very physical and social being, there remains the need for personal prodding and social restraints. Permissiveness is fine for the white middle class, but an oppressed race above all needs discipline.

In the western world today — and what seems like all the world, under western influence — the authority to discipline has been systematically taken away from parents and teachers, and concerned adults (the agents of nurturance and development) and given over to the agents of punishment and rehabilitation (the police, the courts, judges, lawyers, social workers, probation officers, psychotherapists and counselors).

Where discipline (the centerpiece of the instrumentality of socialization) once was essentially preventive, it is now predominantly corrective. Once upon a time, teachers with authority to discipline held classroom decorum conducive to teaching. Today, the inner city teacher, lacking authority to discipline, must spend most of her time trying to get discipline instead of teaching. In many classrooms, about all that goes on there is one continual but futile endeavor to achieve discipline and decorum. We must begin to push to restore discipline to the school but also to the home. Where empowerment of parents and teachers will not suffice, we must provide the help (including personnel) to restore discipline — without which little else is possible.

We must begin to return to the source, to go back and wrap ourselves in a proud and glorious past, not so much to get bogged down there, as to use this new sense of pastness as a springboard for a new and collective future. We must go back as far as precolonial Africa, to find out what served us well in the way of childrearing and the making of honorable adults, to rediscover what we lost that is worth saving that could serve us today.

That is why, in the summer of 1985, we wrote a book, *Bringing the Black Boy to Manhood: The Passage,* calling for the making of the African rites of passage into a mass social movement in African-America. Schools and teachers comprise ideal conduits for sustaining and advancing the rites of passage movement now in progress.

Chapter 9

Community

What we can do to motivate and mobilize the community and its human resources is limited only in the cobwebs of our imaginations, our broken initiative and our chronically thwarted will to act. In the centripetal direction (working from the outside or the community toward the school as center of focus and action), we might initiate varsity *academics* in the manner of varsity athletics long held traditional. Competition in and among schools would then be encouraged.

A recent study widely reported in the media found that black students may do poorly because, unlike whites and other ethnics, black students neglect to study in groups. This would appear to contradict the "afrocentric cognitive styles" theory that black children tend more to learn in groups ("relational" styles versus the eurocentric "analytical" cognitive style), but in fact may be more a product of the fact that study activities are not prevalent enough in black homes and communities on even an individual plane sufficiently to spill over into group life and activities.

Inner city black children are even less likely to gather to play with academic toys and academic children's games. Befitting the social class and orientation of their parents and overall social environment (largely bookless, for instance), their toys are less likely to be academic. When inner city black children gather, as in skating rinks or video malls or poolhalls or playgrounds and basketball courts, it is largely in a non-academic form of play, often punctuated as well in too many cases by acting-out behavior, periodic vandalism, delinquency and destructive aggression.

Such children not only need aggravated adult supervision in a wide array of play activities; they also need more academics in their play activities. Beyond this, we have long believed that black children will in time do better in academic performance (indeed any group performance) where there is the idea of the game and the contest, or conspicuous competition. This results from the oppressed black child's special need for personal and social recognition and a comparative necessity to seek compensatorily that recognition in himself as embodiment. Excelling in games in the manner of athletics not only brings the joys of instant recognition and repair of a damaged self-esteem, but also provides psychological escape from a severe environment of sparse external rewards.

There is talk now of Saturday school in public systems, and extracurricular or community-based "Saturday academies" have cropped up in places as unlikely as Riverside, California. Success activities as well as academics may be provided in Saturday school, but even more than regular weekday school, the Saturday school must be a place of profound enjoyment. There is no need for school to be boring on any given day. There should be regularized rapping and dancing (creatively interwoven and simultaneous with academics.) Children should be required to convert literary passages or biographies of historical figures into rap lyrics and perform them for the class.

The opportunity to participate in dancing could be a reward for a job well done, not necessarily limited to the top students but a reward as well for effort or/and a job well done according to the student's recognizable ability. Any chance that the rewarding of such activities will negatively reinforce divergent or socially unacceptable behavior is readily offset by the magnitude of the potential stimulus to academic endeavor. Work and excellence grow out of struggle and are not necessarily fun, but the fun and the rewards (including recreation and, in later adulthood life, even good wines and fancy meals) are precisely benefits potentially of hard work and excellence, except as weighted by fate or uneven fortune.

Success roles and success activities must be promoted. Success Day, Bankers Day (where bankers come out and try to make banking activities attractive and fun), Parents Day, Pastors Day, Fathers Day and such, would pull these persons, leaders and functionaries alike, into the educational process and the school environment. Although this is done to some extent already, it must be implemented infinitely more, and more enticingly.

It is from such participants, that many of the "mentors" and even "tutors" for children can be enrolled or recruited. However, in the centrifugal (inside out) direction, older children should be encouraged or/and required to tutor younger siblings at home.

Unrelated students and peers also may be enrolled as tutors, helping younger or less able students to learn a given subject. Indeed, since teaching is perhaps the best learning device ever invented, students might be directed to tutor one another as an exercise in academics, even when they do not have superior knowledge, in the way that a child less able overall than another in a sport such as basketball may neverthless show him how to execute something specific such as a sky hook or dunk. Just as a child can show another how to shoot a basketball or hold a bat, children should be instructed in exercises and exhortation to show other kids how to count, how to write, how to speak, how to be informed in whatever way.

Academic peer-group-team-study would or could be preparation and practice for an academic contest. Academic contests not only must be encouraged by school activities, including varsity academic teams; academic leagues should be established in youth groups in the community in the manner of current youth athletic leagues.

Undergirding all school and academic activities should be a spirit and an ideal of service to the community. Children should be instructed to help the elderly: say, run an errand for them, help the handicapped, help the less fortunate in whatever way.

We must not be derailed by such as the recent recommendation of California Governor Wilson that schools foster volunteerism. We do need volunteers — but particularly black ones; for hordes of insensitive, if not racist, white missionary-style volunteers will prove to be counterproductive. Not only in the damage they will do directly, but also in setting back the black community's own need to generate and regenerate out of its own spirit and to promote its own initiatives and its own autonomy. As regards volunteerism per se, our approach must be, even as we battle for funds, at the same time to endeavor to do what must be done with or without funds. We must do our job and fight for funds simultaneously.

Meanwhile, some of the money that is going to be used to train white teachers and token mainstream blacks to work with poor black and ethnic children could go to community-based efforts in those poor communities. We can use the help of organized bodies of white volunteers, but we cannot rely on them, and they cannot tell us what we must do or not do. Nor can they do what we must do for ourselves as black people even if they wanted to. They are like the Big Brothers and Big Sisters programs, or the Boy Scouts, to black male socialization, or like United Way and social service departments to black socioeconomic survival and elevation.

Mr. Wilson called on judges, attorneys and other business and community leaders to volunteer. Already there are 450 volunteers spending six hours a year in low income black and ethnic communities. If their black counterpoints — black judges, attorneys, business and community leaders do not rally to a black-directed program, we are left with armies of part-time white secular missionaries ministering to black children, with readily anticipated socio-psychological consequences offsetting any good they can do.

Indeed, Mr. Wilson's call for volunteers to take the work of teachers eliminated by the budget crisis confirms our own estimation that teachers fully credentialed by today's requirements are not necessary to do the job of educating children. Under Governor Wilson, we may yet see white and black persons without credentials doing what credentialing requirements will not now allow excellent black teachers transferring from other states or districts to do as they are denied licensure for such flaws as not having taken teachers arithmetic or state history, though they intend to teach neither.

In small, segregated southern towns in the Jim Crow era, even without sufficient funds, we turned out children who could read and adapt to life. This is not to say that funds don't matter or that we shouldn't demand even more funds than we do; only that funds will not be enough and that we must not wait for funds, because there are things that funds cannot buy.

Some California schools, e.g. Santa Ana, are beginning to

send a parent along with every fifth grader on tours of local community colleges. Each family is then given a picture inscribed with the words: "I am college-bound."

Here are a few of the many other things that might be done by schools and teachers (or extensions of teachers, collateral personnel, including paraprofessionals). In China, teachers send parents "connection books," so-called, we presume, because they connect the parent and teacher in communication around the child and the child's performance and development, forming what might be called an "educational triage." We must begin to get black children involved in success roles. Manytimes, when you ask black children around the age of eleven or twelve (the age in pre-European Africa when children would ordinarily enter a rites of passage and preparation for adulthood) about their ambitions, many black children today cannot name any, saying they haven't yet thought about it. Perhaps they have but find it too difficult to imagine the possibility of achieving it, and so are ashamed or afraid, embarrassed, to verbalize it.

One of the authors was once a graduate student interviewer of juvenile gang members for the University of Chicago's Youth Studies Center. Subjects consisted of members of some of the toughest gangs in Chicago at the time.

In the interview at one point, we would arrive at the question: "what would you like to be doing ten years from now?" The boys would quickly name such things as physician, bank executive, and the like. The next question was: "what do you think you'll actually be doing ten years from now?" They would then stutter and splutter and finally say something like, "I have an Uncle at the steel mill, and he says I might be able to get on at the steel mill."

These boys needed a bridge between their *aspirations* and their *expectations*. We must give them what psychiatrists have labeled "success roles." Success roles include not only a role that will lead to success, but also the actual process of getting them started on a pathway or process leading them toward success. We can do this in many, many ways. One way is to give the young people "success activities," individually, but also to infuse the community and the daily lives of children in the community with success activities. This is already being done to some extent in the schools, but the more teachers and schools can foment such activities in the community and in the daily lives of the children the more effective they will be.

However, it remains important to point children toward success roles at school as well. Like the teacher who discovered that one of the authors didn't know the ABC's by memory in the second grade, the teacher should require that the student without a clear ambition come back with one the next day and start concretely on the road to that ambition through getting involved in success activities and roles leading toward that end. In the process, many black students may also manage to unravel the problem of unrealistic, star-studded ambitions gleaned from television and the disporportionate fixation on athletic, musical and entertainment stardom.

Children can be helped to realize, additionally, that even a star-studded career, both becoming and being a star, requires long hours of hard work and drudgery between taking bows and hand-clapping. The child who would be a star must learn to stick to unpleasant tasks, where necessary. One of the best devices for learning to do this and daily or nightly work of preparation for success is the performance of chores at home and possibly also at school. Parents, paraparents and parenteachers should encourage parents to assign regular chores to the child. Children should be encouraged to perform chores for their parents and families. They might be organized into auxilliary groups to clean and polish and "police" their nighborhoods and their own or one another's homes.

Although pains must of course be taken to keep children's chores at a properly didactic level and to protect them against abusive or exploitative labor, here again we may come up against child labor laws designed for middle class children but hoisted on low-income children as well. Overzealous labor laws and curfews combine to point the slum child toward a life of idleness, often a major avenue to delinquency and crime. It is better for black youth to be engaged evenings in some suitable work (as most of us were in the not too distant past) than to simply "hang out" and drift into delinquent activities.

Aside from anything done to and for students (and black children in a general sense), it is important to find ways to educate parents — not necessarily in the formal sense of accumulating credentials, though that in itself would be all to the good and a latent by-product of education in social awareness and skills in coping with and enjoying life.

For example, teachers may volunteer or/and earn extra pay similar to bi-lingual salary bonuses to teach what they know to parents. Credits could be given to the parents as incentives, suitable for framing, nay, framed for hanging on the wall, whether parents wish to increase their formal or certified educational attainments or not. Parents also might be given token financial incentives to take the courses or workshops, despite our own ambivalence toward the idea of payment and the need to safeguard against being handicapped or stymied by the fickle snares of remuneration.

Suffice it to say that money is surely useful for its own sake — we must always be alert to discern what we deserve or "to get what is coming to us" — but the black educational problem will never be solved by money alone and, when it comes to black educational uplift, the best things in life will be free or voluntarily gained from mobilizing black humanity even as we forcibly restrain the hands of white social inequity. Finally (in the centripetal direction and as we have intended to suggest elsewhere in these pages), parents should be permitted and encouraged to teach what they know also to teachers: for instance, auto mechanics or related information, cabinetmaking, self defense, or whatever they may know that teachers may need or want to learn.

We might even recruit articulate welfare mothers to tell how to avoid the system of welfare and how they themselves got into it and how they hope to get out of it. If each person 25 or 30 years old simply taught children eight to fifteen what they already know, we'd have improvement in a community where, uniquely in human history, it is expected that the children will not achieve as much as their parents did.

If all else fails, we may need to establish learning zones; or, better yet, "Study Zones." Learning is the result, but to effect a result you must take some steps. We must emphasize the process of learning — studying — and learning is likely to be the result. Too often we wish to have the harvest without plowing the field. Just as we have "no smoking zones," and "drug-free zones," we may need to designate selected areas at certain hours as quiet places in which to study, policing disruptive elements and influences and finding ways, on the other hand, to follow these study hours (like happy hours) with a social or dance or talent show, however informal or impromptu. There is no shortage of talent in the black community. Anybody who doubts this can suddenly elicit individuals in any random, assorted or assembled group, to stand and perform some song or routine. The hidden and untapped talent would amaze you; and so would the results once we decide to harness it in the mobilization of mass black educational excellence.

Chapter 10

Society

As with home (including parental) and community involvement, the involvement of society in the educational process must be accomplished in both directions — centrifugally and centripetally — from the school to society and from society to the school. Society must operate to change the values, practices and processes of the school, just as the school and those concerned with black education must operate to change society, its values, its definitions, its policies and its agendas.

Centripetal

Beginning with societal involvement in the school, we may do well, in the manner of athletics and entertainment, to make the black educational process generally topheavy with the spirit of exhibition and a contest. As the children rehearse, practice and skirmish for *academic* varsity participation or intramural competition and routine course work (modeled after physical education classes), they are brought automatically into group study and group preparation. The child could continue some isolated study just as a lonely basketball aspirant practices freethrows or jumpshots.

Insofar as is possible, educational activities should likewise be conducted as contest or a game or skirmish in preparation for competition. Just as many students do not make athletic varsities, yet learn to live with it, the slovenly academic or artistically uninclined can govern themselves accordingly. Those who can't make the "A" team may make the "B" team, or wait until next year, or join the academic cheering squad or marching band or identify with their team as enlightened spectators in the name of school or class or subclass spirit.

We must have sympathy and compassion, even more than in the past, but we can no longer protect the recalcitrant or reluctant, or even the "slow learner", at the expense of those who can and will learn, anymore than we would think of doing this in athletics. Ironically, we will begin for the first time truly to help slow learners, creating the kind of academic students the basketball teams can be proud of.

In the days when black children in school — though segregated and secluded on sharecropper farms in rural, backwater Southern communities — could learn to read, spelling bees were conventional. In routine classrooms, come rain or come shine, the children in a class would be lined up before the others. To compete to answer the teacher's questions, they would be lined up in casual rank order according to presumed or demonstrated ability.

If one student missed a question, he or she got "turned down" in the line and would have to concede his or her place to the child next in line who, answering correctly, could turn him down. In the end, the best student on a given day would emerge at the head of the line and the worst student would turn up at the foot or the end. Though the general ranking of the students would not change, brisk competition would emerge among individual students and pairs from the head to the foot of the line, although the greatest attention and classroom excitement would focus at the head, where competition is keenest and closest.

We should revive the spellng bees, adding math bees, science bees, and so on, during schooltime and sometimes at night for parental and public display and competition. White mainstream psychologists and educational theorists became so concerned with "protecting the child" from the faintest emotional slight that, in following their narrow-minded script, we have managed to slight black children as a whole.

Black children delight in competition. Competition among black youth was brought to an art form in breakdancing duels and dunking wars, and "showing off" and "playing the dozens" (ritualistic, competitive putdowns demeaning one another's dearest heredity) have long been popular. Theorists consumed with a polyanna mentality in an age of polyanna still lingering though battered by our decadent reality, will counter that the foregoing examples of competition among black youth are but expressions of "pathology." Be that as it may, they suggest nevertheless that black children can survive competition and, when given half a chance and/or half an incentive, delight in competition.

Everything possible is to be done in groups and games, as contests and exhibitions, bringing inherent psychological reinforcement for individual children. Additional and concrete rewards also must be given in some way to every child. The possibility of winning feeds the inner city child's special need for *conscpicuous recognition*. At the same time, its exhibitionary nature permits the children to learn to "stand and deliver," to address the group or crowd and to assert themselves in the face of the crowd or audience situation.

Teachers and teachers aides should take pains to give verbal praise insofar as possible, and other children should routinely applaud the completion of any exercise or designated activity by a classmate. Otherwise, they should conduct themselves during competition like spectators at an athletic contest, limited only by circumstance and polite decorum.

Old-fashioned debates, however informal, should be pervasive; in class, in schoolwide assembly, intramural and varsity academic competition, or wherever and to what extent. The same for oratorical contests. Students should be given every opportunity for public speaking and expession and impromptu writing, in and out of the classroom. This is especially important for black students, due to the collective problem of inferiority complexes, epidemic speech pathology among impoverished youth, white tendencies to rank black children as well as adults rather heavily on how "articulate" they are, not to mention the popularity of preaching, rapping and expressive behavior in black culture.

Continually, in turn, the children should be instructed to write about a subject at hand and, after their writings are placed in a hat or container, to select a slip randomly, read it, and stand and talk about it, then again to write about what they have talked about — how they felt, what they learned, how they saw others, what they liked or didn't about themselves and others, how they and others might improve, retaining all this as part of their diary or log of their journey through the course or semester.

The successful completion of each course should constitute a milestone, buttressed by a ceremony and a celebration in the class. The smallest accomplishment in class should elicit handclapping or praise. Each semester should be punctuated by such exhibitionary activities as informal parades around the school or up and down the streets by students and teachers marching to the beat of impromptu drums and blaring bugles. It is both grandiose and simple. All we have to do is, like the man who would jump high, back up and get a running start by returning to such as once worked for us and, through common sense and ingenuity, reactivating it again to bring our communities alive once more around the idea of personal mastery and educational excellence.

As we suggested in 1975 (at the California Black Educators Conference held in Sacramento and in a paper presented at Langston University's "Distinguished Alumni" ceremonies and sent black leaders and intellectuals around the country), "we must raise excellence in academics to the level of our excellence in athletics and entertainment." "Where is the Arthur Ashe and the Muhammad Ali of the intellectual world?" we asked black leaders and intellectuals.

However, excepting a fair amount of rhetorical appeals to excellence and "quality education," black intellectuals instead would step-up a push for black children to disdain or turn away from their *athletic* excellence. The intellectuals did this on grounds that athletic effort was thwarting academic effort — as if black people can excel in only one thing at a time — and on the implausible theory that an enthusiasm for athletics, once extinguished, would transform itself routinely into enthusiasm for academics.

If an athletic preoccupation is thought to be a problem to black children, we may take advantage of the social precedent for selective autonomy and independence of action or focus in public schools — the "magnet" schools — which may singularly emphasize art or music or whatnot. The magnet school is in large part the model for the all-black male immersion schools. Paradoxically, an opportunity to focus on the education of black children who can't play sports may also rest in magnet schools for athletes. We mean expressly or officially so, as we are aware that pundits will say that many black schools already operate essentially as athletic magnet schools.

There also might be magnet schools for the would-be entertainers, just as there are magnet schools for classical European music. Magnet schools at least suggest that schools do not all have to be doing the exact same thing simultaneously. Just as what schools do is open to change, so also should be their goals and measurements of acceptable educational progress or what education is, its operational definition. However, black educational reform will need far more latitude than this. What's important, or should be, is the maximal educational development of black children in whatever way.

In reality, we will find that a major obstacle or resistance to black education will be white opposition (often well-meaning liberal and mainstream organizations, established institutions or constituted authority). This stems not so much from conscious racism (though some opposition will come from that source) but from the fact that blacks are *in,* but not completely *of,* white society.

National socio-political authority (which generally professes to be color-blind) is and has been almost exclusively designed, authorized and managed by whites. Although existing regulations and procedures are precisely what has failed black children and black people, they will nevertheless be invoked when any alternative attempt is made to resolve the problem. White society does not wish to let black people go psychologically and economically, let alone legally or politically. Also, the black educational problem represents a complex intermixture of poverty and race, of class and race — two factors the affluent white classes are reluctant to change. They may change one of these, to a limited degree, now and again, but not completely, let alone both simultaneously.

For the moment, however, we need not worry too much about this. We have only to be ever aware of the fact that any serious attempt to educate black children, or to change the educational machinery as applied to black children, will sooner or later arouse white opposition. Race in itself may not be invoked, but in the end, there will stand white people opposing the change on whatever basis, though sometimes black poeple will be delighted to speak for them; for example, the recent Assistant Secretary of Education who spoke againt ethnic-specific scholarship aid. However, we will continue here to enumerate our recommendations as if that opposition does not exist.

Suffice it to say that black educational reform will require a certain mimimal autonomy and independence. This includes the opportunity to err or to make mistakes. If white-directed education and experimentation have failed black children, then black-directed education and experimentation — and we don't mean merely education with white-selected black people representing white society and its viewpoints — should have an equal opportunity to fail black children, according to the American way.

Centrifugal

Working centrifugally (from the school outward to society), it is necessary to promote a black agenda. At the same time, we must resist the unwanted agendas of others antithetical to black interests, or black elevation and empowerment. We must take care to erect relevant new social definitions while simultaneously contending for group rewards and life-chances; and, above all, we must shape the collective ethos, the individual character and socio-cultural disposition of the black child. This is the centrifugal direction of the society component of mass motivation and mobilization for black educational excellence.

History clubs and African Clubs should be started in the community and the schools, bit by bit in time to permeate the black existence. Here "African" includes Africans in America, the expectable members predominantly of the African Clubs. There is no need to modify "African" with "Pan-African," to spell it with a "k" or whatnot; the black child, like black and white America as a whole, needs to grow accustomed to using the word "African" as the appelation of Africans in America, just as Chinese are called Chinese, Italians are called Italians, Germans Germans, Japanese Japanese, and so on. In this way, we will begin to bring Africa to the African-American communtiy, relentlessly, as opposed to treating Africa and Egypt as museums to be visited and viewed mainly on international tours.

In this connection, History Marathons and History Decathlons would be held regularly in the schools and throughout the community. Prizes, raffles, and non-monetary forms of recognition for excellence in knowledge of black and African history should be bounteous at these Black History Bazaars.

In addition to History Clubs, there should be Business Clubs in school and communtiy, organized by students and selected mentors; and there should be Political Clubs, Savings Clubs, and clubs devoted to diverse and specific skills such as mechanics, painting, journalism, law, science, medicine or whatnot. Students in these clubs in turn should be organized into teams. Just as athletics has basketball, football and baseball teams, academics can have teams of engineers, scientists, mechanics, and so on organized and competing as teams, even when the activities are typically individualized as in the example of track and field teams. We should also be reminded that the spelling bees, mathematics bees and science bees, mentioned previously in regard to the competition of individuals, should be organized into teams as well.

Meanwhile, teachers and parents should be encouraged, in the early Booker T. Washington tradition at Tuskegee, to project an image of professionalism to youth and start them on the road to respect for elders, good manners and courtesy to all, including white strangers and functionaries, in the routine manner exhibited by Malcolm X and Louis Farrakhan. The manners of Booker T. Washington, the values of Marcus Garvey and the excellence of Dr. DuBois could become one happy mixture of motivation and orientation for the black or African child. No longer can we pompously debate the relative merits of these three strategists, when we have never really tried either one of them.

We do not have to ask permission to begin to do this. We have a right to do this. We have an opportunity to do this in the home and the community, and we can press for opportunities to teach this in the schools, more so than white-designed and concocted sex education courses. Indeed, we should teach the parents about sexual issues such as sexually transmitted diseases (including AIDS) and fertility issues (from the standpoint of black people, according to our own agenda, not according to white society's genocidal population control agenda even as they push for artificial fertility for the white middle class).

If we will teach the parents, the parents in turn will be able to teach the children. This holds also for academic teaching, character development, social manners and across the board. Not every parent will be readily concerned or even potentially interested, but we must start with those who are and do what we can do, on whatever level, getting the ball rolling, expanding and picking up steam as we may find possible as we go along. We must not be discouraged by what we can't do; once and for all, we must have the courage to do what we can.

SOURCE NOTES

1. Reveille for the Public Schools

The independent black school movement suffered, perhaps irreparably, when the black studies movement took its misturn in the early 1970s. See Harold Cruse, "Contemporary Challenges to Black Studies," *The Black Scholar* (May/June, 1984), pp. 41-47; and the book by Maulana Karenga, *Introduction to Black Studies,* Los Angeles: Kawaida Publications, 1983, pp. 350-376; especially chapter 9, "Challenges and Possibilities;" also various articles of our own from 1969-78. We refer to the failure of black studies programs to take practical steps to promote the idea and development of independent black schools as extensions of black studies (in the manner of college and university "laboratory schools") when black studies turned away from its key *community component* as a part of the black consciousness movement's general turning way from social change to focus on self-esteem and self-flagellation.

Black studies turned to a "museum"approach or focus on ancient African history and culture, relating to Africa vicariously and through periodic trips to Africa, rather than bringing Africa to the black community by permeating it with such as African clubs, history clubs and independent black schools. Cf. Nathan Hare, "A Torch to Burn Down a Decadent World," *The Black Scholar* (September, 1970); " The Meaning of Black Studies," in W. Gordon Whaley, Ed., *In These Times: A Look at Graduate Education with Proposals for the Future,* Austin: The University of Texas, 1971, and other works cited herein elsewhere, 1969-1976. Carter G. Woodson's *The Miseducation of the Negro* is a timeless book first published in 1933 and available but largely ignored all the while. When we discovered it in 1962 in the Howard University Libaray stacks, it had last been checked out in 1936. Then somebody reprinted it in 1968, and it was again reissued in 1978 and, now appearing to be in the public domain, has been in print continually since then, distributed by several publishers and revered by the movement generally.

2. Who Are the Children?

Joseph White, *The Psychology of Blackness,* Englewood Cliffs: Prentice Hall, 1984.

W.E.B. DuBois, *Souls of Black Folk,* New York: Signet Books, 1970, and other works in a long and prolific career. See also Allison Davis's now almost forgotten *Children of Bondage,* 1941. Janice Hale-Benson, *Black Children: Their Roots and Cultural Learning Styles,* Baltimore: The John Hopkins University Press, 1986.

Amos Wilson, *The Psychological Development of the Black Child,* 1983. James Comer and Alvin Poussaint, *Black Child Care,* New York: Pocket Books, 1975.

See Nathan and Julia Hare, "Black Women: 1970," *Trans-Action (now Society)*

(Nov.-Dec., 1970), pp. 65-68. Also, various articles and editorial comment in the journal, *Black Male/Female Relationships,* 1979 to 1982, *passim.* Additionally, Nathan Hare, "Will the Real Black Man Please Stand Up?," *The Black Scholar,* (June, 1971), pp. 32-35. Also, "What Happened to the Black Movement?," *Black World* (January, 1975), pp. 20-33; "What Black Intellectuals Misunderstand About the Black Family," *Black World* (March, 1975) pp. 4-15; and "For a Better Black Family," *Ebony* (February, 1976), pp. 62. "The Psychosociology of Sex and Race, *The Black Scholar* (April, 1978), pp. 2-7; "Black Males in Jeopardy?," interview in *The Crisis* (March, 1986), pp. 30-35.

Also, Julia Hare, "Black Male/Female Relationships," *Sepia,* November, 1979, pp. 82. Nathan and Julia Hare, "The African-American Male on Campus: An Endagered Species," Special Report to *The Black Collegian* (April, 1991), pp. 126-130.

Cf. Haki Madhubuti, *Black Men: Obsolete, Single, Dangerous?* Chicago: Third World Press, 1990. Also, *The Final Call,* April, 1991, plus other issues of this superior newspaper since 1988 for information not generally available elsewhere.

William Glasser, *The Identity Society,* New York: Harper and Row, 1972.

"Foreword" by Asa Hilliard in Janice Hale-Benson, *Black Children: Their Roots and Cultural Learning Styles, (op. cit..* See also Kerby T. Alvy, *Black Parenting: Strategies for Training* New York: Irvington Publishers, 1987, for a system proposed by a white psychologist at San Diego State University. We aren't advocating his system as such (though, insofar as it goes, any diet will probably work if you will follow it); we mention his study because its comparative analysis of black and white parenting images, attitudes and practices, reports that rich whites spank their children more than other race-class cohorts do. Alvy's book also proposes to provide "the first empirical substantiation of the phenomenon of traditional black discipline" — pathetically if so, while black intellectuals assimilated to white middle-class ultra-permissiveness and (as adjuncts to white experts and functionaries) the advocacy and imposition of ultra-permissiveness upon the inner-city poor, in the school and in the home.

3. The White Liberal/Moderate Chodehold

Harold Cruse, *Plural But Equal,* New York: William Morrow, 1986, is an excellent discussion of the social history of the integrationist lure, a good supplement to his *Crisis of the Black Intellectual,* New York: William Morrow and Co., 1967 (which took twenty years to write and is widely regarded by black Ph.D.'s as an apt analysis of themselves). Asked in a Yale University black studies audience which college he attended, Cruse, by then a professor at the University of Michigan, replied that he hadn't attended college, that "it would have been a waste of time."

Re. The Rebirth of Great White Fathers: Studies in Frankencense and Myrrh.

Cf. Kenneth Clark, *Children of the Dark Ghetto*, widely regarded in the pre-black consciousness 1960s. Gunnar Myrdal, *An American Dilemma*, 1944.

For information on the Jimmy P case, contact Prof, Jerry West, Chair, Department of Counseling, San Francisco State University, San Francisco, Calif., 94132.

After the predominantly black Oakland, California schoolboard paid a white headhunting firm $20,000 to choose a superintendent for them in 1981 (suggesting that they themselves didn't know how to find one), they booted out the black fellow chosen in his first year as superintendent and replaced him with a Hispanic who then left them for a system containing a higher proportion of Hispanics. Recently, white authorities for the state threatened to take over the district.

4. An Epitaph for Black Studies

For discussions of the meaning and scope of black studies additional to the previously cited works by Harold Cruse and Maulana Karenga, see the John Blassingame, ed., *New Perspectives on Black Studies*, Champaigne-Urbana: University of Illinois, 1971. Also, for a report of the consultation on the black male student for the Portland, Oregon school district, circa 1987, contact the District, or Prof. Robert Green, Director of Research, Cuyahoga College, Cleveland, Ohio. For the baseline curriculum itself (chaired by Asa Hilliard), contact Matthew W. Prophet, Superintendent of the Portland, Oregon school system, reference *African-American Baseline Essays*, Portland: Multnomah School District 1J, Portland, Oregon, 1987; also, Nathan Hare, "Questions and Answers about Black Studies," *The Massachusetts Review*, 1969, pp. 727-735; and "Teaching Black History and Culture," *Social Education*, (April, 1969), pp. 385-88.

For an account of the motivations behind the first black studies strike (believed also to be the longest and most thunderous strike of any kind in American college history), see William H. Orrick, Jr.'s Report to the National Commission on the Causes and Prevention of Violence, *Shut It Down! A College in Crisis — San Francisco State College, October, 1986 - April, 1969*, Washington: U.S. Government Printing Office, June, 1969. The appendix includes the widely disseminated "Conceptual Proposal for a Department of Black Studies," by Nathan Hare, dated April 29, 1968. However, for the seminal account/analysis, see Oba Tshaka, "The San Francisco State College Strike: A Study of the First Black Studies Strike in the United States," *The Journal of Black Studies*, 1983, pp. 15-23; see also the volume put out by Yale University, containing the speeches of a national sample of selected black scholars, circa 1968; also John Blassingame, ed., *New Perspectives on Black Studies*, Urbana: University of Illinois Press, 1971; Nathan Hare, "Conflicting Racial Orientations of Negro College Students and Professors," *Journal of*

Negro Education, (Fall, 1965), pp. 431-34; "Behind the Black College Student Revolt," *Ebony,* August, 1967; "Final Reflections on a 'Negro College," *Black World,* February, 1968; "The Legacy of Paternalism," *Saturday Review,* July 20, 1967; response to Roy Wilkins on the case against separatism, "The Case for Separatism in Black Studies," *Newsweek,* February 10,1969; and other articles from 1967-1978, *ad infinitum.*

For a very insightful analysis of the hiring and promotion of black college and university faculty, see Robert Staples, "Racial Ideology and Intellectual Racism: Blacks in Academia," *The Black Scholar* (March /April, 1984), pp. 2-17. Though covering fifteen *Black Scholar* pages, the article is excerpted from a longer work by Staples on the new intellectual racism and the "arcane ritual" of academic recruitment, selection and promotion of faculty. Nationally prominent black scholars with years of outstanding teaching to their credit, including some as part-time lecturers in the department to which they are applying, will be required to put on a mock lecture supposedly to demonstrate their in-classroom-real-life teaching ability, as part of the ritual assessment to become a core or "tenure-track" faculty member.

In this way, departments will get several lecturers (inviting campus students and off-campus community persons to attend) scot-free (for which they would otherwise have to pay from $ 2,000 to $ 4,000 each). In other features of the ritual, blacks who publish in black-oriented journals are "presumptively dismissed as being unscholarly, containing political advocacy and polemical." For their part, black professors in black studies programs have generally internalized the white notions of scholarship and senior professors will enhance their stature at faculty meetings by demonstrating their knowledge of white administrative rules, directives and conventions.

At a time when white publishers reject other than crossover manuscripts by blacks, black studies professors, including many who have hardly published at all, will look askance at "self-published" works or even those that are not in "refereed" journals. Also, it is better for a candidate to have only a handful of "reports" and a name on a multi-authored article or two than a large number of publications that include articles in popular national magazines (which contaminates the professor as "unscholarly").

Though Staples does not restrict his analysis to black studies, many of his insights nevertheless apply. For instance, the fact that "although blacks are often regarded as skillfull orators and humorous speakers, they may suffer from the negative evaluations of their teaching by white students." One black studies professor was brought before the dean for a "hearing" after he questioned the wisdom or appropriateness of using 1980s white feminist beliefs to call a 1960s Malcolm a X "sexist," thereby killing or defaming a black hero. (Cf. Oba Tshaka, *The Legacy of Malcolm X, Chicago:* Third World Press, 1983).

Many black studies hiring, firing and retention committees will include representation from the white feminist studies department but not vice versa. Not only is it difficult to gain entrance and advancement in black studies programs without lipservice to white feminism, the fact that many of the black professors are "sponsored" by white feminists causes tenure-seeking black militants to quickly alter their views in the direction of white feminism once hired. At the same time, the white feminist departments will hire black female tokens of their own and pressure the black studies department to hire more who in turn may informally control recruitment in black studies through closer and friendlier access to the ears of white feminists in top administrative slots, or the wives and lovers of white men and lesbians there.

Of course, in many other ways, black studies faculty member are increasingly bent toward white ideals and agendas. For early suggestions of white control of black studies, see Haki Madhubuti's *From Plan to Planet,* Chicago: Third World Press, 1973, and *Enemies: The Clash of Races,* Chicago, Third World Press, 1978. Cf. also Charles J. Sykes, *Profscam: Professors and the Demise of Higher Education,* Washington: Regenery Gateway, 1988.

See *Black Issues in Higher Education* for continual accounts and discussions of black concerns on the college and university campuses. Must reading is the California Black faculty and Staff Association *(CBFSA Newsletter,* publisher, Prof. J. Owen Smith, California State University, Fullerton, California; editor, Robert Fikes, California State University, San Diego, California).

5. Popular Misconceptions and Half-Measures

Re: "Multicultural Education: The Mirage of a Rainbow Imperative:"

On the rainbow imperative in society at large, see *The Black Anglo Saxons,* Chicago: Third World Press, 1991. For a tendency of the black middle class generally to place status over substance, see E. Franklin Frazier, *Black Bourgeoise,* Glencoe: Free Press, 1957. Frantz Fanon, *Black Skin, White Mask,* tr. by C.L. Markman, New York: Grove Press, 1967.

For a tendency of black intellectuals, particularly contemporary nationalists, to place symbolism above substance, see Edgar Ridley, *The Neurological Misadventure of Primordial Man,* 1991, first published in *Black Male-Female Relationships,* Autumn, 1982. Contact E.A. Ridley Associates, Philadelphia for the expanded edition. See also Ridley's review of Frances Welsing, *The Isis Papers,* Chicago: Third World Press, 1991, in *Black Book Guide,* April, 1991, for an analysis of the problem of the preoccupation with symbolism (symbolitis) that consumed the black movement in the early 1970s to now. See also the editorials by Nathan Hare, "Wherever We Are," *The Black Scholar,* March, 1971, and "Combatting Black Apathy," *The Black Scholar,* 1973. Robert Chrisman and Nathan Hare, eds., *Pan-Africanism,* New York: Bobbs-Merrill, 1974.

For important discussions of different varieties of myths and misconceptions, see Zak A. Kondo, *Black Student's Guide to Positive Education*, Washington: Nubia Press, 1988, and *Historical Lies and Myths that Miseducate Black People* (1989), by the same author.

6. Final Reflections on the Idea of a Plan

Alexander Meisterlich, *Society without Fathers*. Also, Karenga, *op. cit.*, chapters on the functions of the arts and education.

7. The Plan

For an early statement of the ideology anticipating the current trend toward white usurpation and institutionalized rearing of black children, see Bruno Bettleheim, *The Children of the Dream: Communal Child-Rearing and American Education*, London: Collier-Macmillan, 1969.

A. Harry Passow, ed., *Education in Depressed Areas*, New York: Teachers College, Columbia University, 1963.

Marva Collins and Civia Tamarkin, *Marva Collins' Way: Returning to Excellence in Education*, Los Angeles: Jeremy P. Teacher, 1982. William Glasser, M.D., *The Identity Society*, New York, Harper and Row, 1972.

For additional Guidelines on organizing in the black community, see the two-wolume work by Prof. Oba Tshaka, Vice-President for Organizing of the National Black United Front, *The Art of Leadership*, Richmond: Pan-American Publications, 1990 and 1991.

8. Home

See the Yale University Children's Center report, directed by James Comer.

9. Community

Ruth Sidel, *Women and Child Care in China*, New York: Hill and Wang, 1972.

William Kessen, ed., *Childhood in China*. New Haven: Yale University Press, 1975.

Since the late 1960s, we have found very useful books on education in Africa, particularly South Africa, too numerous to mention, and on Jewish education and its history, both in America and Israel. Books on education in Africa and other countries can be found in varying quantities in just about any library.

Cf. "History of the Philosophy of Education," and "The Influence of Modern Psychology on the Philosophy of Education," in Paul Edwards, ed., *Encyclopedia of Philosophy*, New York: Macmillan Publishing Co and the Free Press, 1967, pp 230-242 and 243-247, respectively. W.E.B. DuBois, *Souls of Black Folk, op. cit.*, introductions by Alvin Poussaint and Nathan Hare. Nowadays, black leaders and intellectuals will think nothing of stating publicly that they don't know the answer to the black predicament and that, moreover, they don't think anybody does. Nevertheless, they do not get out of the way of those who think they know. John Hope Franklin, the distinguished historian, and Washington, D.C. House delegate and ubiquitous television opinionist Eleanor Holmes Norton, and former civil rights leader James Farmer, are a few examples. Recently, a Virginia professor seeking to promote "rites of passage" programs was quoted on the front page of a black weekly as saying "there are no experts among us; we all have our opinions."

Cf. *Axioms of Kwame Nkrumah: Freedom Fighters' Edition*, Kwame Nkrumah. London: Panaf Publications Ltd., 1967.

Nathan Hare and Julia Hare, *Bringing the Black Boy to Manhood: The Passage*, San Francisco: The Black Think Tank, 1985.

Jawanza Kunjufu, *To Be Popular or Smart: The Black Peer Group* , Chicago: African-American Images, 1988. Also, *Building Positive Images and Discipline in Black Children*.

For overall organizing strategies, consult the two-volume work by Oba Tshaka, *The Art of Leadership*, Richmond, Calif.: Pan Afrikan Publications. Volumes I and II, 1990 and 1991, respectively.

Lawence E. Gary and Lee P. Brown, eds., *Crime and its Impact on the Black Community*, Washington, D.C.: Institute for Urban Affairs and Research, 1975.

10. Society

Jake Patton Beason, *Why We Lose: Why the Black Man/Woman Rest Firmly on the Bottom in America, Africa and Elsewhere*, 1989, P.O. Box 09423, Milwaukee, Wisconsin 53202.

Please send me the books checked below.

How to Find and Keep a BMW (Black Man Working)
by Julia Hare   _____ copies at $10.00* each $ _____

The Black Anglo Saxons
by Nathan Hare   _____ copies at $12.95* each $ _____

Bringing the Black Boy to Manhood: The Passage
by Nathan and Julia Hare   _____ copies at $6.00* each $ _____

Crisis in Black Sexual Politics
by Nathan and Julia Hare   _____ copies at $15.00* each $ _____

The Endangered Black Family
by Nathan and Julia Hare   _____ copies at $10.50* each $ _____

The Miseducation of the Black Child
by Nathan and Julia Hare   _____ copies at $10.00* each $ _____

* **Add shipping/handling of $1.50 per book.**

Total amount enclosed $ _____

Send check or money order to:

THE BLACK THINK TANK
1801 Bush Street, Suite 118, San Francisco, CA 94109

Name _____

Address _____

_____

City _____ **State** _____

Zip _____

Please send me the books checked below.

How to Find and Keep a BMW (Black Man Working)
by Julia Hare   _____ copies at $10.00* each $ _____

The Black Anglo Saxons
by Nathan Hare   _____ copies at $12.95* each $ _____

Bringing the Black Boy to Manhood: The Passage
by Nathan and Julia Hare   _____ copies at $6.00* each $ _____

Crisis in Black Sexual Politics
by Nathan and Julia Hare   _____ copies at $15.00* each $ _____

The Endangered Black Family
by Nathan and Julia Hare   _____ copies at $10.50* each $ _____

The Miseducation of the Black Child
by Nathan and Julia Hare   _____ copies at $10.00* each $ _____

* **Add shipping/handling of $1.50 per book.**

Total amount enclosed $ _____

Send check or money order to:

THE BLACK THINK TANK
1801 Bush Street, Suite 118, San Francisco, CA 94109

Name   _____

Address   _____

              _____

City   _____   **State**_____

Zip   _____